'The Faith of a Felon' and Other Writings

✳

'The Faith of a Felon' and Other Writings

✳

JAMES FINTAN LALOR

With an introduction by
Marta Ramón

UNIVERSITY COLLEGE DUBLIN PRESS
Preas Choláiste Ollscoile Bhaile Átha Cliath

First published by
University College Dublin Press, 2012

ISBN 978-1-906359-26-3
ISSN 1393-6883

University College Dublin Press
Newman House, 86 St Stephen's Green
Dublin 2, Ireland
www.ucdpress.ie

Cataloguing in Publication data available
from the British Library

Typeset in Scotland in Ehrhardt by Ryan Shiels
Text design by Lyn Davies, Frome, Somerset, England
Printed in Scotland on acid-free paper by
Bell & Bain Ltd., Glasgow

CONTENTS

INTRODUCTION

Marta Ramón

In 1881 Thomas Clarke Luby, one of the founding leaders of the Fenian movement, began the publication of a newspaper series of recollections in the New York *Irish Nation* with a critique of Alfred Webb's popular *Compendium of Irish Biography*. Luby praised both the author and the writing, but lamented the omission of three important names from the Young Ireland movement of 1848: Fr John Kenyon, Eugene O'Reilly, and James Fintan Lalor. Luby vindicated their inclusion in a revised edition of the dictionary, and proceeded to explain Lalor's significance to his unadvised American readers:

> Anyone who has ever gone over the files of the *old* Dublin *Nation* has found in the columns of that famous journal no more vigorous writing than certain letters of Lalor's. The most nervous and best reasoned articles – 'The Faith of a Felon', etc. in Thomas Devlin [*sic*] Reilly's *Irish Felon*, were from the pen of Lalor. It was he who advocated, in that successor to John Mitchel's *United Irishman*, the rights of Irish tenants, with a force of argument and manly Demosthenic eloquence . . . which (I make bold to say) have not been even approached in a single

speech or article of all those that the 'Land League' has called forth
either in Ireland or America.[1]

Luby was writing at the height of the Land War, when many of
Lalor's ideas seemed to have been resuscitated in a belligerent
campaign for the transformation of tenants into owners of the soil;
a campaign that, as in Lalor's case 30 years before, was linked to a
more comprehensive aspiration for Irish self-government. Unlike
the majority of Irish land reformers, whose demands seldom went
beyond remedial legislation to secure tenants in their holdings,
Lalor had clamoured for nothing less than land nationalisation and
the abolition of landlordism. For this reason he was turned retro-
spectively into the perfect founding father for the Land League,
and Michael Davitt was able to celebrate him as 'the prophet of
Irish revolutionary land reform'.[2] This was so, even though Davitt
himself did not apparently come into contact with Lalor's work
until the land agitation was well under way.[3] But Davitt was not an
isolated example. Lalor's writing, powerful, inspiring, complex,
and also suitably ambiguous, laid him open to appropriation by
various other writers who in the name of different causes tried to
rescue Lalor from oblivion and claim him for themselves. Thomas
Clarke Luby in the article quoted above praised Lalor on behalf of
Fenianism as 'an active rebel against English rule';[4] Patrick Pearse
went further and listed Lalor with Wolfe Tone, Thomas Davis and
John Mitchel as one of the four evangelists of Irish nationalism;[5]
while James Connolly, with far less justification, labelled Lalor the
'Irish apostle of revolutionary Socialism'.[6] For his own part, Arthur
Griffith, in the preface to the first serious biographical edition of
Lalor's work in 1918, praised Lalor for restoring its 'true meaning'
to the notion of 'moral force' by substituting O'Connell's submission with actual passive resistance to British authority, but he
criticised Lalor for prioritising land reform over nationalism.[7]

Lilian M. Fogarty, the editor of the collection, in her introduction proceeded to offer a detailed but strongly hagiographic and some-times fanciful account of Lalor's career, very much in line with contemporary nationalist discourse.

Fogarty's edition, republished in 1947, has provided the template for all subsequent collections of Lalor's writings, although her transcription contains a multitude of small inaccuracies, and her biographical research was superseded by T. P. O'Neill's more rigorous *Fiontán Ó Leathlobhair* in 1962; a work that became widely accessible after its translation into English by John T. Goulding as *James Fintan Lalor* in 2003. Modern scholars, most notably D. N. Buckley, have completed the literature with a systematic study of Lalor's thought, in a declared attempt to 'rescue Lalor from his disciples',[8] and especially challenge the nationalist and socialist tags attached to him. Buckley's work still remains the most rigorous effort to pin Lalor down ideologically, but in the course of his rescue operation, Buckley tends to slide towards the opposite extreme and underestimate Lalor's impact on his contemporaries. He begins by classing Lalor as a secondary character whose 'marginal involve-ment in a variety of movements in the late 1840s, paradoxically, puts him at the center of Irish history'; he rules him out categor-ically as a Fenian forerunner on the common but mistaken grounds that 'fenianism . . . kept its serene distance from anything that smacked even remotely of class conflict'; and he concludes by acknowledging Lalor's 'crucial' influence on the Land War, but stressing the differences between him and Michael Davitt.[9] Buckley's brief and rather pessimistic conclusion merely draws attention to the changes after the Famine in the circumstances and political outlook of the tenant class to which Lalor had addressed himself during the 1840s, and their eventual disappearance at the turn of the century; suggesting perhaps that Lalor's relevance as an agrarian thinker had perished along with them.[10]

The present edition does not intend to offer a radical reassessment of these previous works, but rather to combine the different approaches contained in all of them, in order to offer the reader all the necessary elements to appreciate Lalor's work. The collection includes in chronological sequence every article published under Lalor's signature, from his first letter in the *Nation* in 1847, until his last call to arms in the *Irish Felon* in July 1848. The articles are preceded by a biographical overview of Lalor's career, and followed by an appendix containing two important documents outside the scope of the main selection. The introduction completes O'Neill's biographical research with a new interpretation of the sources and a closer look at the political context, and addresses some of the inconsistencies that Buckley seems to perceive in Lalor's ideological evolution. The collection itself presents a fresh transcription of Lalor's articles as they were originally published in the Irish press, purging misattributed pieces and removing the numerous inaccuracies and small alterations introduced by Lilian Fogarty and handed down to virtually all subsequent Lalor scholars. Whatever ideological affiliation and political significance are attributed to Lalor, it is hoped at least to reintroduce him to modern readers as one of the great Irish writers of the nineteenth century.

II LIFE AND WORK

II.I Early years

James Fintan Lalor was born at Tinnakill, Abbeyleix, Queen's County (now Co. Laois), on 10 March 1807, the eldest of 12 children born to Patrick ('Patt') Lalor and his wife Anna, née Dillon. The Lalors of Tinnakill belonged to the higher echelons of the tenant farmer class; in 1814 Patrick Lalor was the head tenant of over 117 acres of land and several houses belonging to the earl of Castlecoote, which he sublet at a total profit of £438.15.15.[11] By 1832 he leased between 600 and 700 Irish acres from the Earl of Milltown,[12] of which he farmed 500 acres and sublet about a hundred, giving him an estimated supplementary income of £150 a year.[13] Economic success gave the Lalors social standing and access to local leadership. Patrick Lalor had been active in the Catholic Emancipation campaign during the 1820s, but the Tithe War of 1831–6 gave him national renown and promoted his election as MP for Queen's County between 1832 and 1835. The family patriarch was a strong authoritarian figure who demanded exhaustive reports about the affairs of the farm while he was away, and exercised a strict control over the household finances.[14] Little is known about his wife Anna, except that she passed away in 1835, closely followed by one of the Lalor children, Joseph.[15] One of James Fintan's brothers, Richard (1823–93), was to continue the family tradition as an MP between 1880 and 1892; the youngest of the family, Peter (1827–89), emigrated to Australia in 1852, and began a successful political career of his own, first as a mining activist and later as a prominent member of the Victoria Legislative Assembly.

As regards James Fintan himself, most biographical accounts are dominated by the contrast between a vigorous mind and a feeble and deformed body. It is reported that he had fallen from a servant's arms as a child and twisted his spine into a hump. Otherwise he seems to have been physically strong and in relatively good health until his late 30s; significantly, before he entered the public spotlight.[16] Thus, witness accounts may have given a somewhat exaggerated picture of Lalor's physical fragility by focusing on the years leading up to his death.

Whether on account of his health, his physical handicap, or other reasons, Lalor was almost exclusively educated at home. He attended Carlow College for one year between 1825 and 1826, when a severe fit of illness forced him to return to Tinnakill.[17]

According to his biographer, this period at least helped him to develop his writing skills and acquire the rudiments of Chemistry and Law, but he always regretted the gaps in his own education.[18] The extant catalogue of the Tinnakill library, compiled in 1860, certainly does not suggest a particularly erudite level of home schooling: the bulk of the collection is composed of almanacs, works of reference, travel guides, religious tracts, and an extensive section of history books and other staple works of the Irish nationalist canon.[19] A few of the items, however, reflect Patrick Lalor's involvement in agrarian politics and must have been read with particular interest by James Fintan himself: an 1832 report of the House of Lords committee on the payment of tithes containing Patrick Lalor's deposition, the Poor Law reports for 1841 and 1848, and the Devon Commission report on the land question published in 1844. The Lalor library also includes William Blackstone's *Commentaries on the Laws of England*, the source of Lalor's application of natural law and social contract theory to the issue of tenant right.[20]

There is an unproven story in Lalor's biographical lore, that his exit from Carlow College was followed by a short medical apprenticeship with Dr John Jacob at the county hospital in Portlaoise, then with his son after the doctor died in June 1827. Disagreements with his new employer, or a romantic disappointment according to a different version, prompted Lalor to give up his apprenticeship and start off for France.[21] As Lalor never showed any particular connection with the country, it is likely either that the episode never happened, or that Lalor never reached his destination. T. P. O'Neill explains that Lalor worked at a Chemistry laboratory for some time, then was back at Tinnakill by 1831; he was then 24 years old.[22] Little is known about Lalor's activities for the next 14 years. No correspondence for this period, either from him or to him, seems to have been preserved among the family papers except for one letter to his father in 1834.[23] This might indicate that he spent most of his time at home and did not have a wide social circle.[24] Despite this apparent seclusion, however, these were Lalor's most formative years.

On returning to Tinnakill, Lalor soon found himself in the thick of the Tithe War, a movement of agrarian resistance unlike any Ireland had seen before. Whiteboys, Ribbonmen, and particularly Rockites during the early 1820s,[25] had defended the interests of the tenantry through secret organisation and scare tactics; open activism and civil disobedience would now take their place. The bad harvest of 1829 and the sectarian tensions exacerbated by Catholic Emancipation, among other causes, had compelled farmers in various localities in County Kilkenny to become organised under the leadership of the local clergy in order to request abatements in their tithe charges.[26] In Graiguenamanagh, however, the Protestant curate, Luke McDonnell, mismanaged the situation to the point of bringing upon himself a full-blown campaign of passive resistance led by the local Catholic priest, Fr Martin Doyle, which soon spread to other parishes in Kilkenny, Carlow, Wexford and Queen's County.[27] On 10 February 1831, at a meeting for parliamentary reform in Maryborough (now Portlaoise), Queen's County, Patrick Lalor caused a sensation by declaring that he would not pay tithes again; he announced that he would violate no law, but expressed his certainty that if his property was seized, no one among his countrymen would offer money for it.[28] He also proposed a system of mutual compensation for losses, and concluded: 'There shall be a society of friends leagued against oppression and unjust exactions. May I therefore not say tithes are virtually abolished[?]'[29] As resistance degenerated into violence, the authorities were alarmed not only at the disturbances, but at the general success of the resisters. Tithe collection became a laborious and dangerous process; arrears accumulated, and unrest persisted.

Tensions were not defused until 1836, when new legislation substituted tithes with a tax payable by the landlord. The cost was still transferred to the tenants through the rent, but this removed direct contact between tenants and tithe collectors.

As Patrick O'Donoghue points out, the Tithe War campaign was not widespread or well organised enough to match the success of the Land League 50 years later, but it constituted a useful test.[30] It certainly taught Lalor valuable lessons; in his 1881 recollections, Luby recalled Lalor telling him back in 1849 that 'different countries had their different kinds of guerrilla warfare; and that the Tithe War presented a good specimen of Ireland's kind; and . . . that some such movement, gradually developing into regular warfare, should initiate an Irish struggle for independence'.[31] Still Lalor was conspicuously absent from the public spotlight throughout this period; unlike his younger brothers, he is not mentioned in newspaper reports about his father's public appearances.[32] O'Neill concludes that this was owing to disagreement with his father's politics; Buckley attributes it to his family's concern for his health, embarrassment about his deformities, or the fact that he had already come under the influence of William Conner, a pioneering agrarian reformer who campaigned for more radical measures than a reform of the tithe system.[33]

Conner, as Lalor would do later on, upheld the 'industrious classes' as not only the most numerous, but also the most important to the economy of the country, and dismissed Repeal as an intellectual question that paled in importance next to the bread-and-butter issue of tenant right.[34] Against the established principles of laissez-faire economics and the sacred rights of private property – in agrarian terms, the belief that landlords were entitled to manage their property as they saw fit, and the government ought to interfere as little as possible with the 'natural' laws of supply and demand – Conner pointed out that land was a peculiar kind of private property and could not be subjected to the same principles as other commodities. Unlike manufactured articles, the amount of land was finite and could not be multiplied to fit an increase in demand.[35] This limitation gave landlords a monopoly of the raw material, engendered harmful competition and rack-renting, and reduced the tenants' profits to the barest level of subsistence. Since parliament had always agreed to regulate the price of monopolised articles, there could be no objection to legislation which would give tenants a fair valuation of their holdings, and security against eviction. It is on the basis of these demands that Conner has been considered the father of the '3 Fs' – Fair rent, Fixity of tenure and Freedom to sell the tenant's interest – which became the standard programme of land reform after 1850.[36]

Unfortunately, as it happens with many other aspects of Lalor's life during the 1830s, there are no extant written exchanges between the two men to fill in the details of their connection or their discussions on agrarian issues during Lalor's intellectual coming-of-age. However, Conner's vindication of the tenant's supreme natural right, combined with the tactical lessons gleaned from the Tithe War, provide two of the main pillars of Lalor's subsequent programme of agrarian revolution. There is a third pillar, on the other hand, that escapes such easy categorisation: the connection in Lalor's ideological system between agrarian rights and national rights. Some of Lalor's most sweepingly nationalistic passages – 'Ireland her own, and all therein, from the sod to the sky. The soil of Ireland for the people of Ireland, to have and to hold from God alone who gave it'[37] – must be reconciled with some surprising political sympathies, and the combination appears to lend some justification to the theory that Lalor was fundamentally an agrarian reformer driven to radical nationalist positions out of mounting desperation.

II.II Lalor and the Conservatives

The majority of Young Ireland leaders – as indeed, the majority of the politically conscious among the Catholic population – began their political career within the Repeal movement. Lalor, by contrast, started out in violent opposition to it. He took his first public steps in 1840 as the secretary of the Shamrock Friendly Society of Raheen, a temperance club,[38] but his first major initiative, only uncovered by T. P. O'Neill in 1962, was nothing less than a secret offer to Prime Minister Peel in June 1843 to inform the government about the Repeal Association with a view to destroying it.[39] The letter was circulated to Sir James Graham, the home secretary, and Prince Albert himself, but nothing seems to have come of it. For those who are aware of Lalor's reputation as a radical nationalist this seems a shocking move, and every mention must be followed by an explanation. T. P. O'Neill excused Lalor on the grounds of sincerity of feeling and concern for the people's welfare; he held an honest belief that the Repeal agitation was an obstacle to reform by a benevolent government, and he offered himself to help stop it, just as he offered himself to the Young Irelanders later on.[40] Buckley takes the episode as an illustration of Lalor's political flexibility, or his opportunism, explaining that 'his theories were plastic constructs, malleable enough to be moulded . . . to cover *all* of the many factions involved in Irish politics in this period',[41] adding that Lalor spent most of his career 'hawking his ideas about from post to pillar in the (vain) hope that some individual, club, or party would sponsor and help to realise them'.[42] In other words, Lalor was ready to give his support to just anybody who might be willing to implement his agrarian programme.

Both are cogent explanations, even if O'Neill may be overstating Lalor's altruism, and Buckley his political cynicism. However, it may be useful to take a closer look at the context of this letter. At the time that Lalor wrote to Peel, O'Connell had proclaimed the

'Repeal year', and had begun his colossal campaign of monster meetings. With the Repeal Association embarked on a full-throttle effort to achieve their main goal, all other issues including land reform became subservient to it. Throughout March and April 1843 the Repeal Association considered simultaneous proposals from William Conner, Sharman Crawford, John Shea Lawlor and Daniel O'Connell himself.[43] In August O'Connell outlined his own relatively mild programme: obligatory 21-year leases, the possibility for the tenant to have his holding valued by the county surveyor and appeal at the county assizes in case of disagreement, and the right to obtain monetary compensation for permanent improvements on giving up the land. He concluded, however, by denying that any of it could be effected except by an Irish parliament.[44]

At a Repeal meeting in Ballinakill in May, Patt Lalor, in a similar spirit declared that Repeal had to be won before William Conner's ideas could be put into effect.[45] Conner himself found that the Repeal Association was no place for agrarian radicalism. On 18 September he announced his intention to move the Association to declare that 'until our national rights, in the possession of our own Parliament, and of a valuation and perpetuity of his farm to the tenant, be restored to us, we Repealers shall pay no rent, county-cess, rent-charge, tithe, poor-rate, or any other charge out of land'.[46] The consequence was Conner's immediate repudiation by the Association and the elimination of his name from the books.[47] It appears that Lalor and Conner had parted ways some time before this, but Lalor would probably have been on Conner's side on the issue of his proposed rent strike, if not with the rest of his programme.[48] In any case, in the middle of a general Repeal euphoria, and in view of the little inclination displayed by O'Connell to tackle the land question decisively in the foreseeable future, it is not unlikely that Lalor felt frustrated enough to resort to O'Connell's conservative arch enemies.

But there was yet another question drawing Lalor towards the Conservatives and against O'Connell's Liberal allies. The Corn Laws, which established protective tariffs on the importation of foreign cereal, were perceived to set the interests of agriculture against those of manufacture. Radicals and Whigs, with different degrees of enthusiasm, advocated their abolition for the sake of free trade and cheap bread for the working classes; O'Connell himself was an avowed 'abolitionist', and in 1842 had published a pamphlet denouncing the Corn Laws as unjust, oppressive and unchristian, 'the plunder of the poor for the benefit of the rich'.[49] At the same time, he was outspoken on the pernicious effects of the Union on Irish manufactures, and had wedded the Repeal Association to a current nationwide effort to revive them.[50] On the other hand Tories, traditionally associated with the landlord class, opposed the abolition of the Corn Laws on the grounds, among other considerations, that the mass importation of foreign corn that must ensue would annihilate local agriculture.[51] This was added to an abhorrence of the industrial system and its accompanying filth, ugliness and disease, and a celebration of a more wholesome and supposedly happier rural life; these were views that Lalor fully concurred with. In Lalor's economic system, moreover, a prosperous agricultural class was the only possible foundation of general prosperity. Wealth was not created by investing industrial profits on agriculture, but the reverse: a comfortable agricultural population was necessary to create the capital and the market for domestic manufactures.[52]

There is nothing in Lalor's sympathy for the Conservatives or his enmity to Repeal, to exclude a belief in Irish independence. Lalor himself admitted to Peel that he had been 'something *more* than a mere Repealer' before his disgust with O'Connellite agitation drove him towards the Conservative party and its landlord base. What it does show, however, is that for Lalor, as for Conner, the immediate issue of tenant right had priority over less tangible constitutional concessions, especially when these were put forward by a movement he saw as ineffectual and corrupt. When the Famine gave tenant right a life-and-death urgency, and the Irish Confederation emerged as a professedly purer alternative to the Repeal movement, all the pieces seemed to come together in Lalor's own nationalist plan.

II.III Out in the cold

In January 1844 Lalor wrote what was intended as a public letter to the landowners of Ireland, vindicating the agricultural interest and attacking the Repeal press for its stance on the Corn Laws.[53] This letter appears to have been the last straw in a difficult relationship with his father, and shortly afterwards he was obliged to leave Tinnakill for Dublin.[54] It was at this moment that his health began to decline, turning him into the weak, deformed semi-invalid that so many Young Ireland accounts were to describe. By the winter of 1844 he was being treated for chest complaints, probably connected with tuberculosis.[55] In June 1845 he suffered a severe crisis, and described the symptoms to his brother Richard:

On Thursday night I got suddenly and dreadfully bad. Fever – headache – quickened circulation – hurried and laborious respiration – violent pain in the region of the lungs – stoppage of spitting – no sleep. – Continued bad, and growing worse on Friday and Saturday. On Sunday morning got some relief. Its [*sic*] well I did, – for otherwise I would have written to you to say that I was dying. But indeed, for that matter, dying I am. . . . I have, – since writing the last line, – commenced spitting up blood. – This, I believe, is a symptom that admits no doubts.[56]

Despite their quarrels Patrick Lalor was naturally concerned about his son and rushed to his assistance.[57] From March until mid-June 1845 Lalor received a total of £5 from his family to help him along,[58] although he still kept his distance from his father. At this time Lalor was engaged by a gentleman named William Blood to look into the functioning of the Belfast Mont-de-Piété, a charitable pawnbroking institution, with a view to establishing a similar enterprise in Wicklow. By late June Lalor was ready to return his findings: the Belfast Mont-de-Piété was hopelessly insolvent despite its reputation as the most prosperous in Ireland;[59] it would be madness to try the experiment in Wicklow. Once this assignment was finished, as he wrote to his brother, there was little 'of a temporal nature' to retain him in Belfast, but he did have some spiritual matters to settle. Ever since the onset of his illness the previous winter, and especially during the worst times when he felt himself dying, Lalor had been struggling to overcome 'sinful' feelings of bitterness and resentment against his father. After the termination of his employment with William Blood he returned to his confessor, and on 7 August he was finally ready to heal the breach. In the course of a long letter to his father he explained his spiritual struggles and asked for forgiveness, although he still admonished him about his unreasonable expectations and demands on other people, and warned him: 'lead me not into temptation'.[60] With this letter normality seemed restored, and Lalor could corres-pond directly with him about his next professional endeavour. Between October and mid-November 1845 – perhaps ironically for someone with his views about the relative worth of industry and agriculture – Lalor was busy trying to get employment at the Belfast Mechanics' Institute, first as a librarian, and when that failed, as a Chemistry lecturer. He was willing to work without a salary, and only required the Institute to provide him with a lecture room and purchase the materials for a chemical library and a laboratory. This was declined by the directors, however, who preferred to give priority to the actual building and the general library, and Lalor had to give up his aspirations.[61] At the end of the year he left Belfast for Dublin, where his health deteriorated again so severely that he finally asked his father to have him brought back to Tinnakill.[62]

II.IV From Conservative to Confederate

Back to the comforts of home, Lalor's health improved rapidly. By March 1846 he was again turning his mind to politics. The failure of the potato crop the previous autumn, which announced the coming Famine, brought a change in Tory policy regarding the Corn Laws. Late in 1845 Prime Minister Peel introduced a new legislative proposal for a three-year plan of tariff abatements culminating in complete repeal.[63] The bill passed on 25 June 1846, but the Tory party was hopelessly split between protectionists and 'Peelites', and Peel resigned four days later over the defeat of his Irish Coercion Bill, opening the way for Lord John Russell's first ministry.

Throughout 1846 and 1847 Lalor discussed the Corn Laws and other issues in correspondence with his friend John Marnell, a Wicklow farmer who had also belonged to William Conner's circle a few years earlier. Lalor was alarmed at the impending abolition of the laws, and with Marnell's help had attempted unsuccessfully to get in contact with Lord Stanley, the leader of the Tory protectionist opposition.[64] Marnell, however, advised Lalor not to waste time in resisting the inevitable, and focus on tenant protection instead. They also discussed developments in the Repeal movement. Late in July 1846 Young Ireland split from the Repeal Association, and Lalor kept a close eye on the seceders. He declared that he was not a Repealer; he told John Marnell, however, that he had 'half a mind' to join the new party, although he feared their 'imbecility'.[65] However, the following December, when the Young Irelanders

gave up any hope of reconciliation with O'Connell and announced the formation of their own political association, the Irish
Confederation, there was no more time for hesitation.

Fearing that the new organisation would fall on the same
mistakes and vices he condemned in the Repeal Association, and
determined to use this opportunity to steer it in the right direction
before its principles and objectives were publicly declared, Lalor
wrote a momentous first letter to Charles Gavan Duffy, editor of
the *Nation* newspaper and de facto leader of the Young Irelanders.
In this letter Lalor offered two earnest recommendations as conditions for his support. The first was that Repeal should not be its
declared aim, especially to the exclusion of any other: he would
never join an organisation that would ignore the land question or
subordinate it to legislative independence. The second was that no
resolutions should be adopted to confine the new organisation
explicitly to moral force and legal procedures; and he suggested
for the first time that the increasingly desperate tenantry could be
the instrument to force the government's hand:

> Let England pledge not to argue the question by the prison, the
> convict-ship or the halter, and I will readily pledge not to argue it in
> any form of physical logic. But dogs tied and stones loose is no
> bargain. Let the stones be given up; or unmuzzle the wolf-dog. There
> is one at this moment in every cabin throughout the land, nearly fit
> already to be untied – and he will be savager by-and-by. For Repeal,
> indeed he will never bite, but only bay; but there is *another* matter to
> settle between us and England.[66]

By his own account, Duffy did not reject this 'startling
programme' out of hand if it could bring success, but he advised
Lalor to put it to the country through the pages of the *Nation*.[67] In
the meantime, he circulated his letter among other members of the

Confederate Council. Lalor was about to give up hope of hearing from them again, when on 10 March he received a letter from Thomas D'Arcy McGee, the promising new leading writer of the *Nation* and future father of Canadian Confederation. McGee informed him that at least Duffy, John Blake Dillon, John Mitchel, Thomas Devin Reilly and Michael Doheny among the leaders would be disposed to make the land question the main issue in the programme of the Confederation, but *not* to place it above Repeal. As for McGee, he accorded the land question equal importance to Repeal, *only* in Lalor's 'national sense of the thing', and under the exigencies of the Famine.[68] Lalor answered:

> I regret to perceive that you seem to have in some degree misconceived my meaning and intention. . . . I *don't* want to make Repeal subservient to land interests. I don't wish – far from it – to consider the two questions as antagonistic. I wish to combine and cement *the two* into *one*, and so to perfect & reinforce, and strengthen and carry both.[69]

In any case Lalor seemed to have received a warm welcome into the Confederation. At this point, both Lalor and his brother Richard, his closest ally, sent in a subscription of £1 each and their names were added to the membership list.[70] The following month they were admitted into the Confederate Council, and the first of Lalor's public letters appeared in the *Nation*.

II.V Lalor's 'Nation' letters

Lalor's first contribution, 'A new nation: Proposal for an agricultural association between the landowners and occupiers', began as a comparatively mild appeal to the landlords to take their place as natural leaders of the country. Lalor's faith in the Conservatives had been demolished by their about-face on the Corn Laws, and any feeling of deference towards the landlords was being annihilated by their behaviour in the face of the Famine, but at this early stage he was still willing to make concessions to the general policy of his new allies. Lalor had apparently intended a more belligerent text, but felt obliged to adapt his tone to the latest resolutions passed by the Irish Confederation, one of which invited the landlords explicitly to 'take the lead in promoting the welfare of their fellow-countrymen', instead of turning to England in vain for protection.[71] Lalor echoed some of these ideas in his article, but he gave them a radical twist. While the Irish Confederation depended on landlord support as a condition for success and a safeguard against revolution, Lalor looked on revolution as inevitable, and urged the landlords to take their place at its head, or perish at its feet.

The article, however, makes impressive reading for other reasons than this open warning. The countless contemporary debates on the Famine usually focused on concrete political measures, possible immediate solutions to the crisis, with or without including self-government. Lalor made the sweeping claim that society as a whole had already collapsed; that the Irish social order based on the potato was effectually destroyed, and it was time to rebuild it on new grounds. He did not call for a new political constitution such as Repeal might bring about, but a 'social constitution', a new social structure established by the common consent of all classes. In practical terms, and in accordance with Lalor's own views on political economy, this consisted in the creation of a comfortable agricultural class, as the foundation of all other economic sectors. He concluded by cautioning the landlords:

> The principles on which that new system is to be founded must either be settled by agreement between the landowners and the people, or they must be settled by a struggle. . . . If you persevere in enforcing a clearance of your lands you will force men to weigh your existence, as landowners, against the existence of an Irish people. The result of the

struggle which that question might produce ought, at best, to be a
matter of doubt in your minds.[72]

The very day that this letter appeared in the *Nation*, Lalor had a
second instalment ready for publication. In this second article
Lalor explained in detail why in his view it was impossible to create
a manufacturing system in Ireland without first establishing a
comfortable agricultural class to make up its consumer base.[73] This
letter was scheduled for publication in the issue of 8 May,[74] but for
reasons that have not surfaced, it was never printed.

Lalor's second published letter, in the *Nation* of 15 May, was
written in answer to a lecture by Archbishop Hughes of New York.
Hughes had rejected the widespread view of the Famine – especially
in Britain – as a visitation of Providence, and ascribed it to the
inherent vices in the Irish social and political system. Those vices
were so ingrained, however, that Hughes found it impossible to
identify them.[75] Lalor undertook to do this for him. He described
the experience of the typical small tenant farmer, who divided his
land and his labour between a grain crop that paid the rent, and a
potato crop that served to feed him and his family for the year. The
potato crop failed, but the landlord still claimed his rent. The
tenant parted with his whole grain crop in order to pay the rent,
and was left without food or seed for the next harvest. Lalor
accused the landlords of selfishness and hypocrisy, but focused on
the government's catastrophic relief measures and the philosophy
behind them. After the first failure of the potato crop in the autumn
of 1845, Peel's government had bought large quantities of grain for
sale at cost price, and had instituted a public works scheme to help
the Irish poor through the crisis. When his government fell at the
end of June 1846, however, the new Whig prime minister, Lord
John Russell, discontinued these measures. Russell's approach
focused instead on institutional relief through the workhouse

system, to be financed by local taxes rather than imperial government grants.[76] One of the most disastrous aspects of the new legislation was the infamous 'quarter-acre clause'; the stipulation that only tenants holding less than a quarter of an acre of land were entitled to relief. In practical terms, as Lalor denounced, this translated into an obligation for struggling tenants to give up their means of self-support and become 'independent labourers' in order to avoid starvation. The eviction of thousands of these small tenants and the 'consolidation' of their holdings into larger units, coupled with the effects of the repeal of the Corn Laws, would effectively end tillage farming in Ireland. Lalor predicted:

> The agriculture that employs and maintains millions will leave the land, and an agriculture that employs only thousands will take its place. Ireland will become a pasture ground once again, as it was before, and its agricultural population of tillage farmers and labourers will decay and die out by degrees, or vanish and become extinct at once.

This second article is one of the most succinct and perceptive contemporary analyses of the operating causes of the Famine. Although Lalor's figures are problematic and his portrait is rather simplistic, he identifies with remarkable clarity two of the main factors pointed out even by modern accounts to explain mass evictions: the Malthusian view then in circulation that the crisis was the unpleasant but necessary solution to the problem of 'surplus' population, and the incipient substitution of grazing for tillage farming which accelerated in the following years. The definition of this policy as 'clearing away men to make room for brutes' became a standard nationalist catchphrase in the following decades.[77]

Lalor closed this letter in a more menacing tone than he had used in his first, warning the landlords that their behaviour was forcing their victims to choose between submission and resistance.

Before he went into details about his own plans for resistance, he proposed to make a final appeal to the landlords. This was 'A National Council', his third and last letter in the *Nation*, published on 5 June 1847. In this letter Lalor referred to the contemplated formation of a new association of landlords under the name of Irish Council, and made his first concrete proposal: similar committees ought to be formed by tenants and tradesmen, and the three estates ought to meet together as a true national assembly. This was a more revolutionary step than it may appear. Elective assemblies of any kind were forbidden by the Convention Act of 1793, and although Lalor claimed that it was possible to effect this plan without contravening it, the intention was rather to circumvent than to comply with the prohibition.

At this point differences began to become publicly apparent between the writer and his new Confederate colleagues. Ever since the first, warmly encouraging letters from Thomas D'Arcy McGee, Lalor had been corresponding with various members of the Confederate Council and had gathered the impression that they looked favourably on his ideas. But months went by, and there was no public endorsement of him, in the *Nation* or otherwise. And now, while Lalor remained deeply distrustful of any organisation set up by the landlords, the Confederation came forward to offer the Irish Council their most enthusiastic support. With growing impatience, Lalor turned to other ways of influencing public opinion besides newspaper writing.

II.VI The road to Holycross

Lalor's first contacts with the Irish Confederate leaders in January 1847 had been simultaneous with the foundation of two separate tenant-right societies: the Cork Tenant League, whose secretary was William H. Trenwith, and the Ulster Tenant Right Association, whose main patron was the Catholic bishop of Derry, Dr Maginn.[78]

Their final aim was the establishment of a national network of tenant-right societies to agitate for the extension to the whole of Ireland of the Ulster custom, an unwritten rule by which Ulster tenants were guaranteed perpetual tenure as long as the rent was paid, and the ability to sell their right of occupancy to a new tenant. Around the middle of April, Lalor wrote to Trenwith in order to offer his cooperation in organising a tenant league in his own area. As Queen's County was his father's territory, he opted for Tipperary. Meanwhile, week after week he waited in vain for signs of public support from the Confederate leadership. Then, late in June he received a letter from John Mitchel that dashed all his hopes. Mitchel seems to have argued in favour of giving the landlords the benefit of the doubt, and asked Lalor to join the Irish Council alongside the Confederate leaders. This was Lalor's incensed reply:

> If *your* opinions be those of the majority of the acting (I should perhaps say *talking*) members of the Council . . . I scarcely know whether I can call, or consider myself any longer a member of the Confederation. . . .
>
> I respectfully decline to be proposed as member of the 'Irish Council'. You won't help to form *tenant-leagues*? as a *support* or a *check*. I want that one guarantee of the good faith of the Confederation. Under assurance of support from them I made use in my published letters of what must now appear as *cowardly threats*, never meant to be fulfilled. I now understand why and how Ireland is a slave.[79]

This letter also contains one of the most famous if perhaps misinterpreted passages in all of Lalor's writings. Once again he explained to Mitchel:

> I have nothing to do with the landlord-and-tenant question, as understood. . . . My object is to repeal the Conquest – not any part or

portion but the whole and entire conquest of seven hundred years – a thing much more easily done than to repeal the Union. That the absolute (allodial) ownership of the lands of Ireland is vested of right in the people of Ireland – that they, and none but they, are the first landowners and lords paramount as well as the lawmakers of this island . . . these are my principles.[80]

Lalor's aim to 'repeal the Conquest', which nationalist interpretations turned into a revolutionary war cry, had a primarily agrarian dimension, whatever its added political implications. For Lalor the English conquest did not resolve itself merely into a loss of political sovereignty – the focus of the Repeal movement – but the *physical* loss of the land itself, the transference of land ownership from the Irish population to a new elite who held their property titles directly from the English crown. His objective was to return those titles to the Irish population, who could then re-grant them to 'deserving' landlords, or transfer them to the occupying tenants in the case of 'undeserving' ones. In order to do this, the key was not to exercise political pressure on the British government, safely entrenched across the sea, but directly on the Irish landowning class, isolated and vulnerable in the midst of their own tenantry. It was this seamless combination of agrarian doctrine and popular-sovereignty theory that set Lalor apart both from mere tenant-right activists like William Conner and Repeal nationalists like Charles Gavan Duffy, and earned him a place of his own in Irish nationalist thought.

But in June 1847 there was an added sense of urgency to Lalor's plan. Only two months remained before the harvest was gathered and immediately appropriated by the landlords as rent payment. Starvation and mass evictions were already annihilating the small tenant class; if another harvest was taken out of their hands, and no solution was found to keep them in their holdings, soon they would be too few and too weak to challenge either the landlords or the British government. Lalor's letter seemed to have some effect, and in August he was able to report to his brother Richard that after a long correspondence, both Mitchel and Thomas Devin Reilly had agreed to assist him, 'in a mode concerted between us'.[81] Lalor also enlisted the help of Fr John Kenyon, one of the very few members of the Catholic clergy who supported Young Ireland against O'Connell, and Michael Doheny, one of the most advanced members of the Council, and himself a Tipperary tenant farmer. Throughout the summer Lalor and Doheny were busy organising a large public meeting, finally scheduled for 19 September at Holycross, near Thurles. In preparation for it Lalor sent a letter to the editor of the *Tipperary Vindicator*, again explaining the causes behind the Famine and calling readers to secure the attendance of the 'entire population' of their districts.[82] Over 200 people signed the requisition calling for the meeting.[83] A tightly printed placard reminded the labourers:

> The Labourers also, as well as the Farmers, are requested and bound to attend. . . . For if the Farmers obtain security in their holdings, at reduced and fair rents, which will enable them to make improvements, the employment of labour will encrease [*sic*], and the rate of wages will rise. But if the Farmers lose their lands, the Labourers will lose their lives, – or sink into wretched paupers depending on the Workhouse.[84]

Richard Bayly, a local land agent, forwarded the placard to one of the Nenagh resident magistrates and reported: 'The notice has been most extensively circulated, and tenants who promised to pay me rent this day, now decline doing so altogether (although I know them to be well able to do so) and give as their reason, that they intend to wait until they hear what is the result of this meeting.'[85]

Shortly before the meeting, however, there were forebodings of a dangerous lack of harmony among tenant-right advocates. By choosing Tipperary as the focus of his labours, Lalor had trodden on the turf of a publican named P. B. Ryan, who was attempting to establish a Central Tenant League for Ireland with headquarters at Thurles. Early in July Lalor had procured a letter of introduction for him from W. H. Trenwith, but there was no understanding.[86] The week before the Holycross event, Lalor called a preliminary meeting, in Thurles of all places, where resolutions were passed requesting Trenwith's support, but declaring that Ryan's aid 'could only bring discredit, disgrace, and failure on any movement in favour of tenant right'.[87] These were only the rumblings of the coming storm.

On 19 September, over 4,000 people assembled at the Holycross fair green. Most of the audience was composed of comfortable tenant farmers, aside from a few small tenants and labourers. At two o'clock, Lalor and Doheny appeared on the platform. Difficulties began with the task of electing a chairman, as no one in the audience was willing to come forward. Eventually a farmer named William Loughnane agreed to be proposed, and was appointed. Lalor acted as secretary.[88] There had been some disagreement between Lalor and Doheny about the resolutions to be proposed. The central aim of the new league was to be the extension of the Ulster Custom to the whole of Ireland, but there were important differences in tone and intended methods. Lalor had forwarded a sample resolution to T. F. Meagher to the effect that 'Tenant right of the North &c. *is hereby declared to be* the rule custom and tenant right of Tipperary', without reference to the authority of parliament; he was also pushing to have the meeting declare a rent strike.[89] Doheny objected that it was too early to propose such a dangerous policy, and gave him to understand that if certain resolutions were passed he would not attend the meeting.[90] In the

event, Lalor agreed to soften his approach; he made no reference
to rent strikes, and punctuated his resolutions with the usual
references to 'lawful means' and the 'force of public opinion'. But
he did not renounce his vindication of tenant-right as a point of
natural law that ought to be regulated by agreement between the
parties. Two of the resolutions declared:

> That of natural right, on the grant of God, the soil of Ireland belongs
> to the people of Ireland, who have, therefore, a clear vested right of
> property in that soil to the extent of full, comfortable, independent,
> and secure subsistence therefrom, which never could or can be parted
> with, pass, or perish . . .
>
> That the sole and only title that can be pleaded to any right of
> private property in the substance of the soil is merely and altogether
> conventional, and, in order to be valid, must be founded on common
> consent and agreement – be created by contract, and conferred or
> confirmed by the will and grant of the people. . .[91]

Eight resolutions were proposed and passed by acclamation.
Everything went according to plan, until the last resolution was
approved, and Lalor made a final appeal to establish a fund and
secure the consent of the landlords. At this point William Conner,
Lalor's former mentor, came forward and asked to address the
meeting. He went into a long exposition of his theories about
competition for land and rack-renting, until Lalor interrupted
him. Conner persisted in speaking, saying that the resolutions just
approved had an air of 'dubiousness'; Lalor protested that they
had assembled to work, and not to listen to 'long-winded haran-
gues'. The argument fell into mutual personal attack; Conner
accused Lalor and his father of mistreating their own tenants, and
threw Lalor's previous support of him to his face; Lalor retorted
that he had supported Conner until he was 'justly' expelled from

the Repeal Association. Eventually Lalor grabbed Conner by the collar and tried to force him off the platform; Conner still persisted in speaking, proclaiming that tenant-right was a 'delusion'. When a part of the platform gave way in the confusion, Lalor declared the meeting over. Then the audience split between those who stayed to hear Conner, and those who accompanied Lalor to recover at a nearby public house.[92]

Lalor continued working after Holycross, but his projected tenant league never got off the ground. Subscriptions failed to come in, his own father disclaimed publicly all connection with his activities as dangerous and visionary,[93] and the murder of William Roe, a Tipperary landlord, on 2 October allowed his adversaries to put an unpleasant colour on the 'Lalor Doheny school' of tenant right.[94] He was further disappointed, yet again, in the Irish Confederation's response, and his relationship with Doheny deteriorated quickly. Lalor understood that Doheny was committed to his plans; Doheny vindicated his own independence, and declared that he was willing to help Lalor only as far as his opinions allowed.[95] Early in November, Doheny wrote to him encouragingly: after Holycross, the Repeal Association, the Northern tenant leagues and the Irish Council, all had taken up the cause of tenant right.[96] Only a few days earlier, the Council had had a three-day debate under the grand heading of 'meeting of peers and commoners' to discuss different schemes, and in line with the Holycross resolutions, Mitchel had argued for the extension of the Ulster Custom to the rest of Ireland.[97] Lalor lashed back:

> If you consult *Mitchel*, my life for it, he tells you the time [for a rent strike] is *not yet come*! You think it passed.
>
> And you are right. It is too late. It was too late even a month ago. It was too late two months ago. The question should have been taken up and worked when I proposed it in January last. . . .

Oh! but – 'look at the state the question is now in – taken up by the Association! (the devil it is!) taken up by the Irish Council (zounds!) and taken up by – the people of *the North*!' Wherefore, the people of the South should leave it in their hands, and – pay their rents, and go into the work-house, or into the ditch. . . .

Tell your friends of the Confederation, that they have surrendered up their country without a blow. I wish them all a good night, and gay dreams.[98]

II.VII Lalor and Mitchel

Late in November Lalor admitted defeat and returned to Tinnakill, intending to submit to his father's wishes and retire from politics altogether. Politics went on without him, however, and the following January he received an unexpected letter from John Mitchel. Lalor, Mitchel said, had been right about the landlords all along. The Irish Council, on which the Confederate leaders had pinned all their hopes, had turned out to be a sham. Mitchel denounced:

When the subject of tenant-right was broached, they shunned it like poison, and the great aggregate of the 'peers and commoners' after dwindling down by degrees, . . . at last came to the voting and division in a meeting of forty persons, amongst whom were not five landlords. I then made up my mind that all the symptoms of landlord nationality we had heard so much about were merely a screw applied to the English government.[99]

With the outbreak of the Famine, Irish landlords were under attack from all sides. The government's public works scheme of 1846 had been designed as a system of temporary loans to allow the landlords to improve their estates; now the government claimed repayment, and this came to threaten already diminishing incomes due to falling rents and swelling poor-law rates. It was in this context that they decided to establish the Irish Council, to protect their interests and, as Mitchel said, confront the government with a show of strength. But the landlords' enthusiastic approval of the new Coercion Bill introduced at the end of November finally convinced Mitchel that the 'old alliance' had been re-established, and it was time for more revolutionary measures. His new opinions left him without a place in the *Nation*, and in December he abandoned the newspaper in order to set up business on his own. The first issue of the *United Irishman* – Mitchel's emblematic gospel of Irish republicanism – came out on 12 February 1848. For the moment Mitchel merely asked Lalor generally about his views and his future plans; a few weeks later he asked Lalor to join the staff of contributors with one letter a fortnight, at a rate of 30 shillings per letter. But Lalor took this as an insult, and on Mitchel repeating his request, he simply asked him to return to him all his letters on the land question.[100] From then on, direct communication between them ceased, and Lalor's name was never even mentioned in the newspaper.

Lalor had apparently been offended at the small payment offered – 'a salary of 15 shillings a week', as he dismissed it – but the main reason for his resentment was that he accused Mitchel of having appropriated his ideas. Charles Gavan Duffy, who had his own standing feud with his *Nation* co-editor, in his later memoirs made much of this point, turning Mitchel into Lalor's unfaithful disciple.[101] It is undeniable that Lalor made a deep impression on Mitchel and caused a radical change of direction in his political thought; first, by his refusal to depend on landlord support (an almost unheard-of stance in the age of deference and elite politics), and secondly, by his plans to declare a rent strike and sustain it by passive resistance. But Duffy misrepresents the situation on two counts. First, he assimilates the notions of passive resistance and actual insurrection in order to accuse Mitchel of inconsistency; by

Duffy's account, Mitchel had been the most outspoken detractor of physical force until Lalor crossed his path. But Mitchel and Lalor had very different revolutionary plans. Mitchel wanted to provoke a revolution by desperation; Lalor, even on the eve of the Young Ireland insurrection, wanted Irish tenants to seize their rights, and defend them by civil disobedience first, active sabotage work later, and finally, only if needed, 'venture to try the steel'.[102] Secondly, Duffy describes Mitchel's decision to 'intrude' Lalor's opinions on the Confederation as a sudden and almost inexplicable decision.[103] In fact, from the late summer of 1847, when Mitchel and Devin Reilly had agreed to aid Lalor 'in a mode concerted between us', Mitchel began to make suggestions that owed much to Lalor, but also showed that he was more than a mere disciple.

A few days before the Holycross meeting, Mitchel tried unsuccessfully to persuade the Confederation to declare in favour of a strike on both rents and rates; an addition that Lalor could never agree with.[104] Around this time, the *Nation* also began to include occasional references to moral insurrection,[105] and democratic schemes that sounded extremely unlike Duffy, but were consistent with Mitchel's ideological evolution. These were more elaborate plans to seize national sovereignty than Lalor had contemplated. Thus on 25 September, an editorial urged Poor Law guardians across the country – in effect, mostly landlords – to defy government authority and sabotage the Poor Law; refuse to levy new rates in their districts, and use their position to prevent food exports, provide employment to the local poor and mobilise public opinion in favour of universal tenant right.

The main difference between Mitchel and Lalor was the idea that the rates should be boycotted as well as the rents. Rents were charged to tenants, and they supported the landlord class; rates were partially or wholly charged to proprietors, and they supported local Famine relief.[106] A rent strike was an attack on the landlords;

a rates strike benefited the landlords and condemned the poor to starvation. Mitchel's intention at this early stage was simply to attract landlord support and entice them to take their 'natural' place as leaders in the struggle. After his final disappointment, his only purpose was to create chaos and shake the population out of its apathy. As he wrote to Lalor, 'If not in "organization" then in disorganisation . . . there may be help. It is better to reduce the island to a cinder than let it rot into an obscure quagmire, peopled with reptiles.'[107] Lalor never had such an apocalyptic outlook on the path to follow. His frustration and impatience were not directed at the landlords or the people, but at the leaders who stalled month after month instead of taking practical steps to help the tenant population defend itself against eviction.

The moderate sections of the Confederation led by Gavan Duffy opted for long-term plans of popular education and parliamentary agitation; Mitchel opted for no plan at all except martyrdom. Between February and May 1848, while the revolutionary epidemic of the Spring of the Peoples swept across Europe, Mitchel conducted what he called a 'public conspiracy' to rally the population and provoke the government into prosecuting him; he finally got his wish. He was arrested on 13 May and put on trial under the new Treason Felony Act. On 27 May, as Mitchel received a sentence of 14 years' transportation, the *United Irishman* published its last issue.

II.VIII The 'Irish Felon'

Lalor's dejection after Holycross and his decision to give up political activity had not lasted very long. The path of tenant-right agitation was closed for the moment, but he still kept an interest in the activities of the Irish Confederation, especially as revolutionary excitement increased, and he was upset when he discovered that both himself and his brother Richard had been left out of the

Confederate Council for the year 1848.[108] His resentment against Mitchel may also have cooled down; sometime in early May he asked his friend John Marnell for a loan in order to go to Dublin and have an interview with him.[109] Marnell was unable to help, although for Lalor's sake he did not regret preventing the meeting. Finally after Mitchel's transportation, Lalor received an offer that made him leave the comfort of Tinnakill for Dublin once again. John Martin and Thomas Devin Reilly, Mitchel's closest associates, had decided to start a new journal to take the place of the *United Irishman*, literally as well as figuratively; the paper was to be published from the same premises as its predecessor, 12 Trinity Street. John Martin was to be the editor and responsible proprietor, and Devin Reilly, Lalor and Joseph Brenan, a young Cork poet who had also contributed to the *Irishman*, were to be the leading writers. The prospectus of this new journal, defiantly called the *Irish Felon*, declared for national sovereignty, defended the right to own arms and learn how to use them, and proclaimed three of the classic maxims of Irish republicanism: 'all "legal and constitutional agitation" in Ireland is a delusion', 'no good thing can come from the English Parliament or English Government', and 'no good thing comes from [elite] "Leadership".' One additional principle addressed Lalor's particular concerns:

> 5th. That the custom called TENANT RIGHT, which prevails partially in the North of Ireland, is a just and salutary custom both for North and South; that it ought to be extended and secured in Ulster, and adopted and enforced, by common consent, in the other three Provinces of the Island.[110]

The first issue of the *Irish Felon*, on 24 June 1848, carried a long, full-page letter by Lalor to the editor, laying out the principles on which he was ready to lend his cooperation. First, he cautioned that the newspaper ought not to be conducted as a commercial venture, but 'a political confederacy for a great public purpose'; the proprietor ought to have his capital covered, and the staff their expenses refunded, but any profits above this ought to be used to finance the cause. He then proceeded to explain what the cause was, as he understood it. In much the same terms as he had employed when writing to the Confederate leaders the previous year, he emphasised that he did not intend to fight for Repeal, 'in its vulgar acceptation', but in tune with the new times, now he declared explicitly for 'full and absolute independence'. Lalor's language once again made him a favourite author for quotation by later republicans:

> Not to repeal the Union, then, but to repeal the conquest, – not to disturb or dismantle the empire, but to abolish it utterly for ever, – not to fall back on '82 but act up to '48, – not to resume or restore an old constitution, but to found a new nation, and raise up a free people, and strong as well as free, and secure as well as strong, based on a peasantry rooted like rocks in the soil of the land, – this is my object, as I hope it is yours.

Again, republicans were blind to the fact, or chose to ignore it, that Lalor's notion of 'abolishing the conquest' was very much circumscribed to the idea of dismantling the landlord system and turning tenants into proprietors. There was in Lalor's ideological system none of the militant across-the-board egalitarianism that distinguished Irish republicanism after 1848; the *Irish Felon* itself in its prospectus vindicated the franchise for every man who contributed to the state with his taxes, but this did not amount to universal male suffrage. Lalor applied much the same principle to his plan of agrarian justice. The tenant population had a right to the perpetual use of the soil of Ireland, not only because they were

Irishmen, but because they happened to be paying rent. Labourers were Irishmen too, but since they paid no rent, they had no stake in the land and no property claims on it. They had only to hope that the tenants' prosperity would result in more work and better wages for themselves. It did not apparently occur to Lalor that, as John Marnell suggested, a movement by the tenants to claim proprietorship in the name of natural law might prompt independent labourers and cottiers to make similar demands on the tenants themselves.[111]

What Lalor proposed in this first letter in the *Felon* was not in fact an alliance of agricultural classes, but one between town and country. After Mitchel's transportation, the Irish Confederation had adopted a semi-public plan to stage a formal challenge to the government after the September harvest. Clubs multiplied, and members were being urged to provide themselves with arms. But club activity was concentrated in urban areas, with almost no penetration into rural districts; a fatal flaw when the Confederate leaders found themselves trying to rally the Tipperary countryside a few weeks later. Lalor cautioned that the country population would never follow that of the cities into battle for Repeal alone. Repeal was an urban aspiration; the country wanted land tenure above all else. Lalor avoided taking sides openly, but advised the cities:

Between the relative merits and importance of the two rights, the people's right to the land, and their right to legislation, I do not mean or wish to institute any comparison. . . . But, considering them for a moment as distinct, I do mean to assert this, – that the land question contains, and the legislative question does *not* contain, the materials from which victory is manufactured; and that, therefore, . . . it is on the former question, and not on the latter, we must take our stand.

Then, in the heightened atmosphere of June 1848, and free from the need to soften his language for the sake of party policy, Lalor gave full vent to his contempt for the landlord class, 'an outcast and ruffianly horde, alone in the world and alone in its history, a class by themselves'. He insisted that the rights of property of an elite were worthless against the right to life of the rest of the population, and perhaps with some naivety as to the real-life workings of popular revolutions, again pointed to the landlords the only path of salvation if they wished to preserve their property: let them swear allegiance to the Irish nation and consent to hold their titles from it.

The next issue of the *Irish Felon* carried two different pieces by Lalor. The first article, 'The first step – The Felon Club', built on the plan suggested to John Martin the previous week, and made a novel proposal: Lalor called for adherents to a new military organisation which should spread into every parish in Ireland and have the newspaper as its general headquarters. The advantages of such an arrangement were apparent when the IRB established the *Irish People* 15 years later, but unlike the Fenian leadership, Lalor was not interested in a mass movement that could overwhelm the British army in the field; his plan was rather the establishment of an elite of writers, orators and military organisers to take charge of the revolution. Illiterate labourers therefore need not apply: 'It is not the *common* labour, but the *skilled* labour of the country, we desire to engage and organise in this club.' Lalor's appeal continued:

Any one who is qualified to form or lead a company, or a section of pikemen, – or who is willing to head a forlorn hope, – or who is able to address a public meeting, or who is competent to write a paragraph fit to appear in print – any and every such person will be gladly received as a member, and welcomed as a friend and comrade.

They would not proceed with the new organisation, however, unless the country demonstrated its support by producing at least one volunteer in every parish. Five hundred members was the minimum. It is of course impossible to know how many people responded to this appeal, partly because the *Felon* papers have not yet surfaced, but at least 16 letters have been preserved in the Lalor collection at NLI. These present an interesting array of supporters: from prominent English-based Chartists like George Archdeacon, to more or less anonymous correspondents in Ireland and Britain who declared their republican zeal, raised legitimate doubts – 'If by [*sic*] going over to Ireland tomorrow, how would I support myself?'[112] – asked for further instructions, and offered advice. A young doctor's son pointed in the direction that Irish republicanism was to take before long:

> I think it would be well to get a kind of secret organization in every principal town in Ireland. Suppose it to consist of as many members as there are outlets to the town. Each member to devote himself to the study of how he could best take or defend his own part. There need be no oath taken which would I think save it from spys [*sic*] if such happened unluckily to be in it.
>
> The Government tells no one what it is about to do, why then should we disclose our secrets.[113]

Lalor's second article in this issue of the *Felon*, addressed 'To the Confederate and Repeal Clubs in Ireland', lay before his readership the declaration of principles he had sent for circulation among the Confederate leaders in late January 1847, only a few weeks after his first letter to Charles Gavan Duffy. In now familiar terms, he insisted that Repeal was 'absurd and impracticable', and went on to argue his point meticulously. This article is noteworthy for including Lalor's famous image of the land question as the railway engine that could drive Repeal to success. Two additional elements, however, make this a crucial centrepiece in Lalor's work. First, in suggesting to the Confederation the path to follow he hinted at a possible method to undermine British authority, one law at a time, by what he termed 'moral insurrection'. There was no single law that could serve to vindicate Repeal, but the principles he stated were curiously fitting for a rent strike:

> The law you select for assailing must have four requisites: – first, it must form no part of the moral code; second, it must be essential to government . . . one the abrogation of which would be an abrogation of sovereignty; third, it must be one easily disobeyed; and fourth, difficult to enforce; in other words, a law that would *help* to repeal itself.

In any case, the collapse of British authority ought to be followed by a substitute national government, and he did not hold out any hope of success while leadership was allowed to rest on the landlords. He consented, for the moment, to follow the Confederation in the 'experiment', as long as the landlords agreed to admit the tenants into their counsels, and negotiate with them some form of security of tenure. But there was a '*dernier resort*' that he meant to put to the Confederation in due course.

The second and by far most important contribution of this article to an understanding of Lalor's thought is the declaration for the first time of his position within Irish nationalism, summed up in two principles: civic nationalism, and independence that could be partially surrendered into a federal structure. Civic nationalism, as opposed to ethnic nationalism, does not vindicate national sovereignty on the grounds of racial, cultural or religious specificity, but on the simple basis of the consent of the governed, according to the principles of natural law. If 'every distinct community or nation of men is owner of itself; and can never, of right, be bound to submit to be governed by another people', Lalor maintained, such a community was therefore morally entitled to disregard 'usurped' authority and resist any attempt to enforce it.

Refusing to acknowledge the legitimacy of British authority was the standard republican position after 1848, although Lalor's role in this development was a rather roundabout one. The consolidation of republicanism as a political option after 1848 in fact began with John Mitchel's sensational campaign in the *United Irishman* and his attainment of martyr-hero status after transportation. In effect, it was Mitchel who taught republican enthusiasts to treat British authority as a charade. This letter, however, places Lalor at the origin of Mitchel's own conversion and lends some justification to Duffy's *exposé* of their master-disciple connection.

However, other aspects of Lalor's programme, at least in this early formulation, were not adopted by later republicans. In January 1847, independence was not for Lalor the final goal, but a necessary prelude to a federal arrangement. The federal solution to Repeal had already been debated during the early 1840s, and was perhaps Lalor's attempt to conform to the majority feeling about the importance of the 'golden link of the crown'; the IRB made no such concessions. Still, it required only six months of general revolutionary excitement, and the end of government forbearance, to bring Lalor forward from his January 1847 positions.

Early in July the government issued a warrant for John Martin's arrest. Initially Martin went into hiding for strategic reasons; the commission assigned to judge him was about to be dissolved, and he hoped that his trial would be delayed for several months while a new one was appointed. On Friday 7 July, as the commission adjourned, the police broke into the *Irish Felon* office, confiscated all papers and manuscripts, and seized the entire impression of the paper for that week.[114] The editors brought out a clandestine second edition, and the following day Martin gave himself up while Lalor proclaimed from the *Irish Felon*:

> THE English Government is determined, it seems, to conquer and carry this office by quick assault or wearing siege. . . . The Castle and Conciliation Hall, the Castle and the Confederation, the Castle and one hundred Club-rooms, may stand together in this island; – the Castle and THE FELON office cannot stand together – one or other must give in or go down.

Lalor made an urgent call to put into effect the plan he had suggested in the first issue of the *Felon*: the newspaper ought to become a joint-stock company, owned collectively by hundreds of activists in the cause. He also tendered a special invitation for some 'English Chartist of known talent and honesty' to become a co-editor. The same issue of the paper included, hastily, what was intended as the first half of a new declaration of Lalor's principles: 'The Faith of a Felon'. In another seminal article, Lalor explained the history of his connection with the Young Ireland leadership, and summed up his own plan in four steps. The first two, along the usual lines, insisted that tenants ought to refuse payment of all rent exceeding their surplus profits, and resist eviction. But for the remaining two Lalor went much further than he ever had:

> 3. That they ought further, *on principle*, to refuse ALL rent to the present usurping proprietors, until the people, the true proprietors . . . have, in national congress or convention, decided *what* rents they are to pay, and to *whom* . . .
>
> 4. And that the people . . . ought to decide . . . that those rents shall be paid *to themselves*, the people, for public purposes . . .

Lalor was aware that some people agreed with the first half of his programme but rejected the second. However, this was precisely what might turn a rent strike from a simple means to cope with hardship, into the assertion of a fundamental right. Those who accepted only the watered-down version of this plan, Lalor warned, 'diminish and degrade it down from a *national* into a mere *class* question. In the form *offered*, it would carry independence – in the form accepted, it will not even carry Repeal'.

Then Lalor went on to challenge the landlords' legal claims to property, by dissecting the notion of private property itself. Lalor began by dismissing William Blackstone's classical criterion of 'first occupancy' as a basis for property claims. On the one hand, 'occupancy' was a vague an artificial principle, 'never respected and never pleaded' in settlement processes. On the other hand, the notion of 'private property' extended only to what a person had actually produced, and therefore it did not include land. The soil belonged to the whole population, its *use* to be distributed by common consent. When families developed into more complex communities, this common consent had to be codified into law, just like any other right, but the people remained 'lords paramount', and retained the right to change the conditions of occupancy at any time. Contrary to classic conservative thought, in Lalor's scheme tradition was no foundation of right; as he argued, 'no generation of living men can bind a generation that is yet unborn'. In order to make the arrangement a permanent one, then, land distribution should be carried out according to the interests of the majority. This was manifestly not embodied by the present system of land tenure, which had been established by conquest and arranged for the benefit of a mere 8,000 individuals. Lalor concluded with an urgent call for the people to abolish this system, 'or be themselves abolished'.

This was Lalor's last public exposition of his theories. Two more articles saw the light before the *Felon* was definitely suppressed: 'Resistance' on 15 July, and 'Clearing Decks', on 22 July. 'Resistance' was prompted by the government's simultaneous onslaught on the *Nation*, the *Felon* and the *Tribune*, the three mouthpieces of the Confederation. On this occasion Lalor went into the reasons why their struggle – which he dated from the beginning of the Tithe War – had traditionally failed to produce results. He ascribed it to lack of constancy under pressure, and exhorted his readers to meet government persecution with an obstinate blow-for-blow strategy. Accordingly, he announced that a new journal – or three new ones – were to be established to take the place of the assailed ones, and again called for subscribers.

Lalor's last published article, 'Clearing Decks', came out just as the government declared the suspension of habeas corpus and began the wholesale arrest of Young Ireland leaders, forcing the Irish Confederation to prove that they were prepared to put their pikes where their mouths had been for the last five months. In keeping with this spirit, Lalor warned his readers to ignore calls to caution from false leaders, and exhorted some one among them to make a beginning. Perhaps to the detriment of Lalor's legacy, the closing sentence of this article came to embody his whole reputation for his nationalist disciples: 'Who strikes the first blow for Ireland? Who draws first blood for Ireland? Who wins a wreath that will be green for ever?'

II.IX The '49 Conspiracy

Lalor's final articles in the *Felon* were published against the background of frantic activity by the Confederation to stage a revolutionary response to the government clampdown. Martin had given himself up on 8 July; Gavan Duffy was arrested on the 9th; Meagher and Doheny followed on 10 and 11 July respectively, although they were released on bail shortly afterwards. On 17 July Lalor summoned his brother Richard urgently to Dublin, and asked him if possible to bring their brother Peter along. Apparently the intention was to have Richard take charge of the rising in Queen's County.[115] The regular Confederate Council, an unwieldy body of over 20 people, was not suited for organising secret concerted action, so on 21 July delegates from all the Dublin clubs met in order to appoint an executive revolutionary committee. Lalor came forward for election, but was narrowly defeated by Thomas Devin Reilly. The rest of the seats in the committee went to John Blake Dillon, T. F. Meagher, Richard O'Gorman and T. D. McGee.[116] In the course of the meeting Lalor tried to have the clubs declare for a rising by 8 August. Meagher and Dillon objected that they could not make such definite pledges, but they promised to do their best to ensure it. The suspension of habeas corpus the following day, however, precipitated matters against their will. Forced to make their move, the Confederate leaders spent a full week trying to coordinate the clubs and rally popular support for an insurrection; an increasingly hopeless enterprise that finally collapsed on 29 July, when Smith O'Brien's motley forces were dispersed by police fire at the Widow McCormack's house in Ballingarry.

Around Monday, 24 July, Lalor left Dublin for Tipperary. He spent the next few days moving about, trying to mobilise the population and reportedly suggesting to his listeners that raiding the local big houses might be a convenient way to provide themselves with arms.[117] On Friday 28 July, however, the authorities caught up with him, broke into the house where he was being sheltered, and took him to be confined at Templemore. From Templemore he was removed to Nenagh, and two weeks later he finally joined the majority of the state prisoners in Dublin's Newgate prison. He had been brought in order to testify at John Martin's trial and clear him of responsibility for his own articles in the *Felon*. Martin's attorney had second thoughts, however, and

Lalor never appeared before the judges, even for his own trial: his feeble health could not stand imprisonment for any length of time, and by the autumn his fellow prisoners were urging the authorities to release him lest he would die on their hands. Finally in mid-November they consented, and Lalor was set free.

It was this almost moribund Lalor that Gavan Duffy had seen in Newgate for the first time. He was still recovering at the house of a Dublin friend in Capel street when Thomas Clarke Luby met him at the end of the year. Lalor was still confined to his sickbed, but as full of projects as ever. Meeting him again shortly afterwards, Luby heard with some scepticism about Lalor's plans for a revolutionary army, able to supply their own equipment and containing representatives of every trade in each regiment.[118] A few months into their acquaintance, however, Lalor sent for Luby particularly in order to ask his cooperation in a more feasible plan; one that he had attempted time after time since 1847.

After the collapse of the Irish Confederation in the July insurrection, many former Confederate clubs had continued their activities as secret revolutionary cells, but there was no master organisation to coordinate their efforts. In March 1848, Joseph Brenan, Lalor's *Felon* associate, on his release from prison called a meeting of about a dozen former Confederates, including Luby. They considered their present circumstances and the course to follow, and finally agreed to join the secret society started the previous autumn by Philip Gray, former secretary of the Swift Confederate club. Now Lalor greeted Luby as a fellow member of this new conspiracy, and asked his cooperation in what he considered the essential public side of revolution: a new nationalist journal. Picking up where he had left off with his old *Felon* scheme, he intended this newspaper to be a joint-stock business owned by members and sympathisers.[119] Lalor hoped to persuade Gavan Duffy to be the editor-in-chief, now that he too had been released from prison, but Duffy had his own journalistic plans, and so did some of Lalor's fellow conspirators. In April 1849 Joseph Brenan announced that he had himself become the editor of the Dublin *Irishman*, a radical democratic journal originally founded to replace the suppressed *Nation*.[120] Duffy for his own part had decided to resume publication of the *Nation* and focus once again on parliamentary politics. He had no confidence whatever in revolutionary methods, especially after the events of the previous year, and declined Lalor's offer.[121]

Agreement was no greater among the conspirators regarding their plans of military action. In May 1849 a number of prominent state prisoners, John Martin among them, were about to be transported. The more intrepid members of the secret society decided to make a rescue attempt. Lalor believed that the Dublin organisation was not strong enough to sustain it and was firmly opposed at first, although a few days later he came round and did his share of organising and rallying members. Everything came to a halt at the very last minute, however, when John Martin himself wrote to dissuade them.[122] This incident gave way to tensions between those who still wanted to bring the revolution to a head as soon as possible, including Joseph Brenan, and those like Lalor who preferred a more calculated strategy. Finally they compromised by fixing the September harvest as a date for the rising. In June, Lalor recruited Luby for a tour of the southern districts in order to spread the secret organisation and publicise the newspaper project. It was this tour, and especially their visit to Fr Kenyon in Templederry, that afforded the main topic of Luby's newspaper recollections.

But Lalor's absence from Dublin left the impatient spirits free rein to pursue other daring projects before their September deadline. Queen Victoria was due to visit Ireland in early August; Joseph Brenan intended to make the celebrations in her honour the signal for a Parisian-style revolution in the streets of Dublin, followed by a retreat to the mountains, possibly even with the Queen as hostage.[123] A party of 150 men assembled one night to try and abduct the Queen, but they were frustrated by the unexpected arrival of a police patrol. More dissensions followed. Lalor was in Limerick while this was taking place, but on hearing of the plan and its outcome he rushed to do some damage control. He called a general meeting of the secret society on 5 September in Clonmel. Despite the patent lack of coordination between the different branches, it was decided to launch a simultaneous rising on the night of 16 September in Cork, Limerick, Clare, Kilkenny, Cashel, north Tipperary, Cappoquin and Dungarvan.[124]

But this scheme was only slightly more successful than the 'Queen's affair' had been. The night of 16 September different parties of would-be insurgents proceeded to their assigned locations. Some had instruction to wait for other groups, and then launch a joint attack on their assigned targets. But owing to coordination breakdowns and the arrest of some of the leaders, many waited in vain for hours and finally returned home empty-handed.[125] The only revolutionary disturbance of the night was Joseph Brenan's attack on the Cappoquin police barracks; an incident that resulted in the death of one policeman, but barely made headlines in the contemporary press. Lalor had charge of Cashel; like many others, he waited all night for a sufficient number of volunteers to assemble, and when this did not happen, he simply dismissed his troops.

The failure of the '49 insurrection was his final bitter disappointment. In its aftermath he sent Duffy the following letter from Clonmel:

My Dear Sir,
I don't know whether you are informed, – but I suppose you are partially so – that the '*Public Press*' was to have been published on Saturday-week last, the 15th, as announced by private circulars; and

that it failed to appear because the numbers – and they were immense – who had pledged themselves to support it deserted at the last moment, and refused or failed to come forward.

I have now either to retire and remain mute, or give my pen to some existing journal; and am desirous to know whether the 'Nation' wants me. I can't tell how far I could be of service to it or you; or whether you and I could fully or efficiently agree. We must settle that. As to being of service to Ireland, such as it is, I give it up. The coffin-lid has closed on the last hope of the living generation.

I hope for an answer at your earliest spare moment. Put your letter under cover to Miss O'Ryan, Bagwell Street, Clonmel.

Faithfully yours,
James F. Lalor.
C. G. Duffy Esq[126]

According to O'Neill, Duffy was willing to take Lalor in, but a few weeks later Lalor had recovered a little of his optimism and again embarked on setting up his own newspaper.[127] However, his labours over the past few months and his all-night vigil at Cashel had made a dent in his health, and the onset of winter, as seemed to be the pattern, brought a relapse in his bronchial troubles. This time sickness had the upper hand; he died in Dublin on 27 December 1849.

III LALOR'S LEGACY

For such a 'marginal' figure as Buckley described, and if O'Neill's report of Lalor's funeral is accurate, Lalor had attained consider-able prominence at the time of his death; an empty hearse drawn by six horses headed the procession, followed by Lalor's pallbearers and a crowd that occupied the whole length of O'Connell Street. After a short parade through the city centre, Lalor's coffin was taken on to be buried at Glasnevin cemetery.[128]

The following decades would demonstrate the actual depth and extent of Lalor's influence. Like Thomas Davis, Lalor lived in turbulent times, left a short but impressive written legacy, and died too young to develop his ideas across a wider temporal frame. What his role would have been in the crucial tenant-right years following the Famine can only be guessed. But his status as a pioneer was vindicated both by Gavan Duffy – if chiefly as a stick to beat John Mitchel – and the die-hard republicans who came together years later to form the Fenian movement.[129] In between, Thomas Clarke Luby carried the torch from his short-lived *Tribune* newspaper (1855–6), a predecessor of the IRB's *Irish People*, whose third issue carried the following editorial:

> *All the land of Ireland belongs to the People of Ireland, in the aggregate, to be distributed and made use of just so as best may serve the happiness, prosperity, peace, and security of the People of Ireland.* . . . land differs from all other 'possessions' in being incapable of becoming the absolute 'property' of any individuals. Men can 'own' only what, by their labour and skill they raise out of the land, and what, by their labour and skill, they construct upon it. But the land itself is the Nation's alone, and the Nation may, when it likes, resume every acre of it for the purpose of a re-distribution.[130]

There were fundamental differences, however, between Lalor and his republican disciples. Most importantly, Fenian doctrine disregarded Lalor's goal of effecting a thorough social revolution from its agrarian foundations, and went back to the Repeal movement's simpler tenet that self-government would open up the way for every other reform. That said, the Fenian plan for an eventual land redistribution was even more radical than Lalor's. According to James Stephens's explanation:

> The Irish State would, we held, purchase all landed property save that belonging to those who had taken up arms or conspired in any way against the revolutionists, while those who favored us or remained neutral in the struggle would be more or less indemnified by being allowed to sell their estates.[131]

In other words, while Lalor tried to console 'good' landlords with the prospect of getting back their lands under title from the Irish republic, Fenianism offered only monetary compensation for their inevitable loss. Then, there was no hint that Lalor's 'present occupiers' would retain first claim in the redistribution process. Fenian writers asserted that 'arms and land' were the most valuable possessions of a free people. However, they also pointed out that tenants were not the only or even the worst oppressed class, and asked: 'Are the labouring poor of this country content to be thus for ever outcasts and paupers? Shall they never possess as much of their native soil as would sod a lark, while strangers occupy thousands of acres?'[132]

At the time that these lines were written, Famine deaths, emigration and mass clearances had decimated the numbers of cottiers and small tenants, while the Encumbered Estates legislation of the early 1850s had enabled struggling landlords to sell their properties in order to pay off debts. As Lalor had predicted, this was accompanied by the consolidation of small holdings into larger farms and the switch from tillage to grazing. Large and middling tenants with some capital to spare came out the winners. Economic security in turn brought social conservatism and an attachment to constitutional rather than revolutionary nationalism; these new tenants were no friends of the IRB. But all this was shaken by the next major crisis in Irish agriculture: the bad harvests of the mid and late 1870s. With the fall in agricultural profits and renewed threats of eviction, agrarian outrages increased, and Michael Davitt famously stepped in to organise the Land League of Mayo in August 1879. This was followed by the foundation of the Irish National Land League the following October, and the escalation of agrarian agitation into a fully fledged and perfectly organised Land War. It was at this point that Lalor's teachings seemed to have been vindicated and put into operation, and he was mentioned as a seminal influence both by members and adversaries of the League. Davitt's acknowledgement of Lalor as 'the prophet of Irish revolutionary land reform' has already been noted. On the opposing side, in 1887 Henry Brougham Leech, Unionist professor of law at Trinity College Dublin, with a wealth of quotation pointed accusingly at Lalor's *Felon* doctrines as the source of the Plan of Campaign.[133]

But Lalor's writings were still only available in their original newspaper form. It was not until 1895, in the context of the nationalist revival, that the first published anthology appeared in print with a preface by John O'Leary. T. G. O'Donoghue, the editor, hoped that a favourable reception would enable this to become the first in a series of 'really national and really literary' works.[134] This hope seems to have been disappointed; only one additional work, P. J. McCall's *The Fenian Nights' Entertainments* (1897), features in the catalogue of the National Library of Ireland.

Other Lalor anthologies followed, however. Lalor's agrarian doctrines were no longer relevant at the turn of the century, after the successive land acts of 1881, 1885, 1887 and 1903 had first given security to the tenants and then allowed them to purchase their holdings with state assistance. But nationalism and socialism remained hot topics, and Lalor was posthumously enlisted into both causes. Lalor's presumed socialism was upheld by the Socialist

Party of Ireland in *The Rights of Ireland and The Faith of a Felon*, *by James Fintan Lalor*, introduced by James Connolly. Around the same time, in December 1915 and March 1916 respectively, Patrick Pearse published 'Ghosts' and 'The Sovereign People', where he examined Lalor's doctrine on land ownership and national sovereignty; he was reportedly seen reading Lalor's 'Clearing Decks' some time before the Easter Rising.[135] The year 1918 was the high point, with the publication of both Lilian Fogarty's *James Fintan Lalor* and the volume *Collected Writings* edited by Nathaniel Marlowe. Marlowe's anthology was in turn recycled in 1973 as *Readings from Fintan Lalor* by the Belfast Republican Press Centre.

Lalor's significance nowadays is mainly as a historical figure, to be included in accounts about the land question and the Young Ireland movement. But there is another aspect of his legacy that never fails to be mentioned by contemporaries, yet is hardly ever given more than passing attention by modern scholars; and that is the purely literary excellence of his work. Luby and O'Leary, both discerning literary critics, praised him highly for his vigour and clarity, while Joseph Brenan gave him the following obituary:

> He was a grand theorist, and his web of thought was ever of the finest tissue. He only wanted ground whereon to plant his lever, and he would have shamed Archimedes. . . .
>
> As a political writer he was never excelled. Without reference to the wisdom of his remarks, I fearlessly assert that his style was the perfection of its species. . . . Word rose on word, sentence on sentence, as blocks in a temple. . . .
>
> Ireland has produced no abler man, no truer patriot; none, I assert, who better deserves a wreath which shall be green for ever.[136]

It is not necessary to have a peculiar interest in the problems Lalor expounds, or agree with his arguments and proposed solutions, to be immediately drawn in by the sheer force of his words. Lalor's argumentation is thoroughly logical, but never detached from the human tragedy behind the Famine; it is intense, but never overly violent or melodramatic. Even the slight mannerisms – particularly his taste for alliteration and the endless numbered sequences of points – only keep the reader engaged and make for an instantly recognisable style. Literary studies tend to forget journalism in favour of the classic genres of fiction, poetry and drama, but newspaper articles and editorials have the added value of combining literary merit with historical immediacy; Lalor's articles offer an outstanding example of both.

Notes

1 *Irish Nation*, 3 Dec. 1881.

2 Michael Davitt, *The Fall of Feudalism in Ireland* (London and New York, 1904), p. 79.

3 T. W. Moody, *Davitt and Irish Revolution, 1846–82* (Oxford, 1981), p. 208.

4 *Irish Nation*, 3 Dec. 1881.

5 In the essay 'Ghosts', *Collected Works of Padraic H. Pearse: Political Writings and Speeches* (Dublin, n. d.), p. 240.

6 James Connolly, *Labour in Irish History* (New York, 1919), p. 121.

7 Lilian Fogarty, *James Fintan Lalor: Patriot and Political Essayist, 1807–1849* (Dublin, 1918), p. x.

8 J. Joseph Lee, *The Modernisation of Irish Society, 1848–1918* (Dublin, 1973), p. 172, in David N. Buckley, *James Fintan Lalor: Radical* (Cork, 1990), p. 8.

9 Buckley, *James Fintan Lalor: Radical*, pp. 1, 89, 91.

10 Ibid., p. 92.

11 Rent roll of Patt Lalor, *c.*1814, Lalor Family Papers, National Library of Ireland (hereafter NLI) MS 8570/1.

12 Joseph Leeson, the fourth earl, who had married the Lady Dowager Castlecoote in 1828.

13 *Second report from the Select Committee of the House of Lords, appointed to inquire into the collection and payment of tithes in Ireland, and the state of the laws relating thereto; with the minutes of evidence, and an appendix, and index. 1831–2,* p. 62; Buckley, *James Fintan Lalor: Radical*, p. 10.

14 Thomas P. O'Neill, *James Fintan Lalor*, trans. John T. Goulding (Dublin, 2003), pp. 29–30 (hereafter quoted as O'Neill, *James Fintan Lalor*).

15 O'Neill, *James Fintan Lalor*, p. 9.

16 *Irish Nation*, 3 Dec. 1881.

17 O'Neill, *James Fintan Lalor*, pp. 23–4.

18 Ibid., p. 25.

19 Lalor Family Papers, NLI MS 8570/2.

20 Buckley, *James Fintan Lalor: Radical*, pp. 30–2.

21 O'Neill, *James Fintan Lalor*, p. 27; John O'Hanlon, and Edward O'Leary and Matthew Lalor, *History of the Queen's County* (2 vols, Dublin, 1907–14), ii, p. 700.

22 O'Neill, *James Fintan Lalor*, p. 27.

23 Lalor Papers, NLI MS 8563.

24 Buckley makes a similar point to explain the lack of sources for the period 1827–31 (*James Fintan Lalor: Radical*, p. 16).

25 See James S. Donnelly, *Captain Rock: the Irish Agrarian Rebellion of 1821–1824* (Madison and Dublin, 2009).

26 Patrick O'Donoghue, 'Causes of the opposition to tithes, 1830–8', *Studia Hibernica*, no. 5 (1965), pp. 7–28; pp. 9–10.

27 Ibid., pp. 10–11; Patrick O'Donoghue, 'Opposition to tithe payments in 1830–31', *Studia Hibernica*, no. 6 (1966), pp. 69–98; p. 70.

28 John O'Hanlon, Edward O'Leary and Matthew Lalor, *History of the Queen's County*, II (Dublin, 1907–14), pp. 653–4; also quoted in Buckley, *James Fintan Lalor: Radical*, p. 11.

29 O'Donoghue, 'Opposition to tithe payments in 1830–1', p. 73.

30 Ibid., p. 74.

31 *Irish Nation*, 17 Dec. 1881.

32 O'Neill, *James Fintan Lalor*, p. 31.

33 Buckley, *James Fintan Lalor: Radical*, p. 16. William Conner of Inch, Co. Kildare, was the out-of-wedlock son of General Arthur O'Connor, the United Irishman, and a cousin of Feargus O'Connor, the Chartist leader. For details about his life and career see George O'Brien, 'William Conner', in *Studies: An Irish Quarterly Review*, vol. 12, no. 46 (June, 1923), pp. 279–89.

34 William Conner, *True Political Economy of Ireland* (Dublin, 1835), pp. 2–3; *cf.* Lalor's 'A new nation', published in the *Nation* of 24 Apr. 1847, item no. 1 in the present collection.

35 Conner, *True Political Economy of Ireland*, pp. 15–16.

36 O'Brien, 'William Conner', p. 287.

37 *Irish Felon*, 24 June 1848.

38 Lalor Papers, NLI MS 340, no. 73; O'Neill, *James Fintan Lalor*, p. 34.

39 James F. Lalor to Sir Robert Peel, British Library, Peel Papers Addenda, MS 40530, ff 399–400v. See item A in the Appendices.

40 O'Neill, *James Fintan Lalor*, pp. 39–40.

41 Buckley, *James Fintan Lalor: Radical*, p. 27 (emphasis in the original).

42 Ibid., p. 28.

43 *Nation*, 22 Apr. 1843.

44 Ibid., 19 Aug. 1843.

45 O'Neill, *James Fintan Lalor*, p. 36.

46 *The Times*, 21 Sept. 1843.

47 *Nenagh Guardian*, 23 Sept. 1843.

48 See 'The faith of a felon', *Irish Felon*, 8 July 1848. Lalor dated his belief in rent strikes before the outbreak of the Famine, although he repudiated the idea of withholding the poor rate, and in 1847 proclaimed that Conner had been justly expelled from the Repeal Association as a dangerous man.

49 Daniel O'Connell, *Observations on Corn Laws; On Political Pravity and Ingratitude; and on Clerical and Personal Slander, in the Shape of a Meek and Modest Reply to the Second Letter of the Earl of Shrewsbury, Waterford, and Wexford, to Ambrose Lisle Phillipps, Esq.* (Dublin, 1842), p. 3.

50 C. D. A. Leighton, *The Irish Manufacture Movement, 1840–3*, Maynooth Historical Series, no. 5 (Maynooth, 1987), pp. 17–18, 23–4.

51 For scholarly discussions on Conservative thought on the repeal of the Corn Laws, see Michael Lusztig, 'Solving Peel's puzzle: repeal of the Corn Laws and institutional preservation', in *Comparative Politics*, vol. 27, no. 4 (Jul., 1995), pp. 393–40, and Anna Gambles, 'Rethinking the politics of protection: conservatism and the Corn Laws, 1830–52', *The English Historical Review*, vol. 113, no. 453 (Sept., 1998), pp. 928–52.

52 'A new nation: Agricultural Association for the Protection and Promotion of Agriculture. To the Landowners of Ireland, no. 2', Sequel to Lalor's first letter in the *Nation*, unpublished. Lalor Papers, NLI MS 340, no. 58. Item B in the Appendices.

53 Lalor Papers, NLI MS 340, no. 59.

54 O'Neill, *James Fintan Lalor*, p. 43.

55 Ibid., pp. 43–4.

56 J. F. [James Fintan] Lalor to Richard Lalor, 25 June 1845, Lalor Family Papers, NLI MS 8563.

57 Jerome Lalor to James F. Lalor, 13 Feb. 1845, Lalor Papers, MS 340, no. 87.

58 J. F. Lalor to Richard Lalor, 19 June 1845, Lalor Family Papers, NLI MS 8563.

59 J. F. Lalor to Richard Lalor, 25 June 1845, Lalor Family Papers, NLI MS 8563.

60 James F. Lalor to his father, 7 Aug. 1845, Lalor Family Papers, NLI MS 8563.

61 J. F. Lalor to his father, 12 Nov. 1845, Lalor Family Papers, NLI MS 8563.

62 J. F. Lalor to his father, n.d., Lalor Family Papers, NLI MS 8563; O'Neill, *James Fintan Lalor*, pp. 45–6.

63 Michael Lusztig, 'Solving Peel's puzzle', pp. 400–1; See also Peter Gray's detailed account in *Famine, Land and Politics: British Government and Irish Society 1843–50* (Dublin, 1999), pp. 107–25.

64 Lalor Papers, NLI MS 340, nos 117, 118.

65 John Marnell to J. F. Lalor, 6 Nov. 1846, Lalor Papers, NLI MS 340, no. 119.

66 J. F. Lalor to Charles Gavan Duffy, 11 January 1847, quoted in Fogarty, *James Fintan Lalor: Patriot and Political Essayist*, pp. 4–5.

67 Charles Gavan Duffy, *My Life in Two Hemispheres*, 1 (London, 1898), p. 236.

68 [Thomas D'Arcy] McGee to J. F. Lalor, 8 March 1847, Lalor Papers, NLI MS 340, no. 108.

69 J. F. Lalor to T. D. McGee, 13 March 1847, Lalor Papers, NLI MS 340, no. 61, quoted in O'Neill, *James Fintan Lalor*, pp. 131–2.

70 *Nation*, 20 Mar. 1847.

71 Ibid., 10 Apr. 1847. For Lalor's intentions see J. F. Lalor to Charles G. Duffy, 18 April 1847, C. G. Duffy Papers, NLI MS 5757, no. 25.

72 'A new nation', item no. 1 in the present collection.

73 'A new nation: Agricultural Association for the Protection and Promotion of Agriculture. To the Landowners of Ireland. no. 2', Lalor Papers, NLI MS 340, no. 58. Item B in the appendices.

74 Answers to correspondents, *Nation*, 1 May 1847.

75 *Nation*, 1 May 1847, reprinted in Fogarty, *James Fintan Lalor: Patriot and Political Essayist*, pp. 128–30.

76 Most histories of the Famine discuss government relief policies; see for instance Peter Gray's extensive treatment in *Famine, Land and Politics*. For a shorter summary see D. George Boyce, *Nineteenth-Century Ireland: The Search for Stability* (Dublin, 1990), pp. 109–15.

77 See for instance *Irish People*, 31 Dec. 1864.

78 Thomas P. O'Neill, 'The Irish land question, 1830–50', *Studies: An Irish Quarterly Review*, vol. 44, no. 175 (autumn, 1955), pp. 325–36; p. 333.

79 Fogarty, *James Fintan Lalor: Patriot and Political Essayist*, pp. 42–5.

80 Ibid., pp. 43–4.

81 J. F. Lalor to his brother Richard, 21 August 1847, Lalor Family Papers, NLI MS 8563.

82 *Tipperary Vindicator*, 24 July 1847. Item no. 4 in the present collection.

83 Ibid., 18 Sept. 1847.

84 Outrage Reports, Tipperary, National Archives of Ireland (hereafter NAI) 27/1695–2532, Carton 1470.

85 Ibid.

86 W. H. Trenwith to P. B. Ryan, 8 July 1847, Lalor Papers, NLI MS 340, no. 159.

87 *Nenagh Guardian*, 18 Sept. 1847.

88 *Nation*, 25 Sept. 1847; O'Neill, *James Fintan Lalor*, pp. 73–4.

89 T. F. Meagher to J. F. Lalor, 25 Sept. 1847, Lalor Papers, NLI MS 340, no. 142. Emphasis in the original.

90 Michael Doheny to J. F. Lalor, n. d., Lalor Papers, NLI MS 340, no. 27.

91 *Nation*, 25 Sept. 1847. The full text of the resolutions is given in Fogarty, *James Fintan Lalor: Patriot and Political Essayist*, pp. 47–9, and reprinted in O'Neill, *James Fintan Lalor*, pp. 163–5.

92 *Nenagh Guardian*, 22 Sept. 1847.

93 *Tipperary Vindicator*, 29 Sept. 1847; *The Times*, 15 Oct. 1847.

94 *Nenagh Guardian*, 16 Oct. 1847.

95 Michael Doheny to [J. F.] Lalor, n. d., Lalor Papers, NLI MS 340, no. 32.

96 Michael Doheny to [J. F.] Lalor, n. d., Lalor Papers, NLI MS 340, no. 31.

97 *Nation*, 13 Nov. 1847.

98 NAI, Official Papers, 1848/104–145, no. 105.

99 Fogarty, *James Fintan Lalor: Patriot and Political Essayist*, p. 121.

100 *Irish Nation*, 17 Dec. 1881.

101 Duffy, *My Life in Two Hemispheres*, I, p. 247.

102 'The faith of a felon', *Irish Felon*, 8 July 1848.

103 Duffy, *My Life in Two Hemispheres*, I, pp. 238, 242.

104 O'Neill, *James Fintan Lalor*, p. 76.

105 James Quinn, *John Mitchel*, UCD Press Life and Times New Series (Dublin, 2009), p. 22.

106 In the case of holdings valued at £4 and less, the whole rate was assessed to the landlord. When the value exceeded this limit, the tenant made the payment, but could recover half the amount as a deduction on his rent. This was a controversial arrangement, however; see for instance 'Rents and Rates', *Nation*, 1 Jan. 1848.

107 Fogarty, *James Fintan Lalor: Patriot and Political Essayist*, p. 123.

108 James F. Lalor to [C. G. Duffy], n. d. [*c.*April 1848], Lalor Papers, NLI MS 340, no. 60.

109 John Marnell to James F. Lalor, 8 May 1848, Lalor Papers, NLI MS 340, no. 135.

110 *Nation*, 10 June 1848.

111 John Marnell to James F. Lalor, 29 March 1847, Lalor Papers, NLI MS 340, no. 128.

112 'A Connaught rebel' to the Editor of the *Felon*, 5 July 1848, Lalor Papers, NLI MS 340, no. 17.

113 James O'Carroll to [Joseph Brenan], n. d., Lalor Papers, NLI MS 340, no. 146.

114 J. F. Lalor to Richard Lalor, 9 July [1848], Lalor Family Papers, NLI MS 8563.

115 O'Neill, *James Fintan Lalor*, p. 87.

116 *Nenagh Guardian*, 21 Oct. 1848; see also O'Neill, *James Fintan Lalor*, pp. 88–9.

117 O'Neill, *James Fintan Lalor*, p. 90.

118 *Irish Nation*, 31 Dec. 1881.

119 Ibid.

120 *Irishman*, 21 Apr. 1849.

121 Duffy, *My Life in Two Hemispheres*, I, pp. 315–17.

122 *Irish Nation*, 28 Jan. 1882.

123 Marcus Bourke, *John O'Leary: A Study in Irish Separatism* (Tralee, 1967), pp. 25–6.

124 Ibid. p. 26.

125 *Irish News*, 4 Apr. 1857.

126 James F. Lalor to C. G. Duffy, 26 Sept. 1849, Charles Gavan Duffy Papers, NLI MS 5757, pp. 215–16.

127 O'Neill, *James Fintan Lalor*, pp. 116–17.

128 Ibid. p. 118.

129 *Irishman* (Dublin), 3 Nov. 1877.

130 *Tribune* (Dublin), 17 Nov. 1855.

131 *Chicago Tribune*, 26 Nov. 1883.

132 *Irish People*, 13 Aug. 1864; 1 Apr. 1865.

133 Henry Brougham Leech, *1848 and 1887: The Continuity of the Irish Revolutionary Movement* (London, 1887), preface. In turn, Leech credited Philip H. Bagenal for the rediscovery of Lalor's writings.

134 *The Writings of James Fintan Lalor*, The Shamrock Library (Dublin, 1895), p. xxiv.

135 O'Neill, *James Fintan Lalor*, p. 122.

136 *Irishman*, 16 Mar. 1850.

'The Faith of a Felon' and Other Writings

:+:

LALOR'S ARTICLES

CHAPTER I

'The Nation', 24 April 1847

A New Nation

proposal for an agricultural association between the landowners and occupiers, no. I

To the landowners of Ireland

Tenakill, Abbeyleix, April 19

I address you, my lords and gentlemen, from a great distance – the distance that separates you from the people; for I am one of the people. This is a disadvantage of some account, and might be discouraging at a season more settled. But I know that in periods of peril, when distress and disaster are present, and danger and dread are in the future, men are allowed to assume rights which must lie in abeyance during ordinary times. This is my reason and right in addressing you – that I am excited and authorised by the feelings and emergencies of the occasion. This is my claim to a hearing – not that I ask it in my own cause or in that of the class I belong to; not that I urge it for [the] sake of the masses of men who are unable to ask it for themselves; but that I claim a hearing and crave to be heard on your own behalf – on behalf of your own interest, and honor, and existence, as owners of that soil on which thousands now are famishing to death for want of food.

My general object in addressing you is that of calling public notice, if I can, to the full extent of the effects which I think must inevitably follow fast on present events, if the course of those events be not checked or changed. All the facts I possess I have considered and counted in one view together, in their connexion and consequence, and inferred the result. This is a task which few others, I fear, have undertaken, nor is it any matter of surprise. Within sight and sound of this dismal calamity, amid the actual horrors of every passing hour, it is scarcely possible to look far into the future, or take thought and care for remote results. In the presence of famine men are blind to its effects. It is doing its work in the dark, and no watch is set or warning raised. From every house and every voice throughout this land there is but one cry now – the cry for food. Food for to-day and for to-morrow – for this year and the next. But not all the clamour and outcry that has been raised throughout Ireland during the last few months has added a single pound to the supply of food either for this year or the next. What men were unable to do, they set about doing; what they were able to do, they left and are leaving undone. For something else is wanting, and requires to be provided, besides food for to-day or to-morrow; else a revolution is at hand. A revolution of the worst type and character – not such as when a nation breaks up under armed violence, to re-unite and rise in structure as strong as before; but such as when it falls in pieces, rotting to a final and fetid ruin.

Besides the general object mentioned, I have a particular and more definite purpose, which will develope itself as I proceed. It would be useless to state it formally before it can be fully understood. Though I write more especially for you, my lords and gentlemen, landowners of Ireland, yet I write also for the public; and shall address myself to either, as occasion may seem to demand.

The failure of the potato, and consequent famine, is one of those events which come now and then to do the work of ages in a day, and change the very nature of an entire nation at once. It has even already produced a deeper social disorganisation than did the French revolution – greater waste of life – wider loss of property – more than the horrors, with none of the hopes. For its direction still seems dragging downwards, while her revolution took France to the sun – gave her wealth, and victory, and renown – a free people and a firm peasantry, lords of their own land. It has unsettled society to the foundation; deranged every interest, every class, every household. Every man's place and relation is altered; labour has left its track, and life lost its form. One entire class, the most numerous and important in Ireland, has already begun to give way; and is about being displaced. The tenant-farmer of ten acres or under is being converted into an 'independent labourer'. But it is accomplishing something more than mere social derangement, or a dislocation of classes. It has come as if commissioned to produce, at length and not too soon, a dissolution of that state and order of existence in which we have heretofore been living. The constitution of society that has prevailed in this island can no longer maintain itself, or be maintained. It has been tried for generations; it has now, at least, been fully and finally tested; and the test has proved fatal. It was ever unsound and infirm; and is now breaking to pieces under the first severe experiment, an experiment which that of any other country would have easily withstood. Nor heaven nor human nature will suffer it to be re-established or continue. If the earth, indeed, with all things therein, was made wholly for the few, and none of it for the many, then it may continue; if all creation was made for you, my lords and gentlemen, and none for us, then it may continue; if men are bound to live on for ever, slaves to a dominion that dooms them to toil, and cold, and hunger, – to hardship and suffering in every shape; if they have no right even to life except at another's license, then it may continue; if they be bound to submit in patience to perish of famine and famine-fever, then it may continue. But if all have a right to live, and to live in their own land among their own people; if they have a right to live in freedom and comfort on their own labour; if the humblest among them has a claim to full, secure, and honest subsistence, not the knavish and beggarly subsistence of the poorhouse, then that constitution cannot and it shall not be re-established again. When society fails to perform its duty and fulfil its office of providing for its people, it must take another and more effective form, or it must cease to exist. When its members begin to die out under destitution, – when they begin to perish in thousands under famine and the effects of famine, – when they begin to desert and fly from the land in hundreds of thousands under the force and fear of deadly famine, – then it is time to see it is God's will that society should stand dissolved, and assume another shape and action; and He works His will by human hands and natural agencies. This case has arisen even now in Ireland, and the effect has already followed in part. Society stands dissolved. In effect, as well as of right, it stands dissolved, and another requires to be constituted. To the past we can never return, even if we would. The potato was our sole and only capital, to live and work on, to make much or little of; and on it the entire social economy of this country was founded, formed, and supported. That system and state of things can never again be resumed or restored; not even should the potato return. A new adjustment is now to be formed, or to form and develope itself; a new social order to be arranged; a new people to be organised. Or otherwise that people itself is about to become extinct. Either of these is inevitable; and either is desirable. In condition and character and conduct, a stain to earth, a scandal among the nations, a shame to nature, a grievance to Heaven, this people has been for ages past – a dark spot in the path of the sun. Nature and Heaven can bear it no longer. To any one who either looks to an immediate directing

Providence, or trusts to a settled course of natural causes, it is clear that this island is about to take existence under a new tenure; or else that Nature has issued her decree – often issued heretofore against nations and races, and ever for the same crime – that one other imbecile and cowardly people shall cease to exist, and no longer cumber the earth.

The power of framing a new order of arrangement is in your hands, my lords and gentlemen, if you choose to exercise it. The work of reconstruction belongs of right to you, if you have the wisdom and the will to do it. It is in emergencies and occasions like the present, rather than in ordinary and settled times, that a national aristocracy is required; and if they be not worthy of such occasions they are worthless altogether. It is a time like this that tries and tests the worth of a class, as it tests the worth of individual men. Not to time should the task be committed, nor to chance; not to the government of England, which is incompetent to the case; not to the parliament of England, where you are made a mark for pelting at; nor to the desperate remedies of men whom you have, yourselves, made desperate. Ireland demands from you now something more than her present dole of daily food, – a mode and system of procuring full food for herself. She looks to you for this, – that she be not condemned to live as a beggar on public alms, nor as a pauper on public works and poorhouse rations; but aided and enabled to find or form a mode of making her own bread in all future time by free, unforced, and honest labour. She has lost her means of living; she requires some other, more sufficient and secure than those she has lost. Her demand, in full and fine, is for what is of more effective worth and weight than all the political constitutions that were ever fashioned; – for what senates or sovereigns cannot make or unmake, but men must make for themselves, – her demand is for a new SOCIAL CONSTITUTION under which to live. This is the task you are called on to undertake, the work you are wanted to do, or forfeit your footing in this island of ours – a work to which political constitution is little in comparison and light in importance. Political rights are but paper and parchment. It is the social constitution that determines the condition and character of a people, – that makes and moulds the life of man.

We are now living in the midst of a social anarchy, in which no man knows with certainty what he is, or what he can call his own. Never was government or guidance more necessary to a people; but government or guidance there is none, for the one great purpose needed. An extreme and extraordinary case has arisen, – one that seldom arises in modern times; – and not to be judged or treated by any ordinary law. A new structure of society has to be created; and the country has a right to require of you to counsel, and conduct, and lead her; because you own her soil; because your own worth and value are in question; – your own interest and position involved and committed; because the work cannot so speedily and safely be done without your aid; because in some respects and some degree you are considered specially chargeable with the calamitous crisis that has occurred; because your rights of ownership are thought by numbers to be the main or only obstacle to the creation at once of a sound system of social prosperity and happiness, which would be found by the natural energies and social instincts of mankind, if those energies were left free to act, and not fettered or interfered with by your claims of dominion; and finally, because you ought of right to be, – where you have never chosen to be – at the head of this people. And at their head or at their side you must now stand, else your aid will not be taken. On other terms it will not now be accepted; and the work will be done by other hands than yours. You are far less important to the people than the people are to you. You cannot act or stand alone, but they can. In the case that has arisen, the main power is in their hands, and little in yours. Your power of position has departed. You cannot re-form and reorganise a whole people without their own consent and co-operation. You cannot act against them, – you cannot act without them. They can do what is wanted of themselves, and without your assistance. They have the will and may learn the way. A dissolution of the social system has taken place. The failure of the potato was the *immediate exciting* cause. Into the *predisposing* causes it is needless for the present to inquire. There was no outrise or revolt against it. It was not broken up by violence. It was borne for ages in beggarly patience, until it perished by the visitation of God in the order of nature. A clear original right returns and reverts to the people, – the right of establishing and entering into a new social arrangement. The right is in them, because the power is in them. The right lodges where the power lodges. It is not a case to which governments or parliaments are competent. The sole office and duty of government under the circumstances is that of supporting the destitute, and maintaining public order during the period of transition and re-organisation. Should it attempt doing more than this, it will be assuming a power which it does not possess, and cannot even make an effort to exercise without committing injustice, doing injury, and suffering defeat. With the great body and mass of the people, in their original character and capacity, resides of necessity the power, in its full plenitude, of forming or falling into a new form of organisation, – a new mode of living and labour. Your aid, my lords and gentlemen, is most desirable, if accorded on terms, and in a mode which would be thought likely to contribute to general benefit and happiness. On other terms or for other objects, – with a view to your own personal interests alone, and on terms to assert and secure your own position at any cost to the country and community, – if offered on such views and terms, your service and aid will not be accepted; and the present condition of anarchy will be protracted by strife and struggle, terminating possibly in violent convulsion, from which you, at least, would

come out the losers, whoever might be the winners. To ensure
against such a contingency, it is necessary that you should now
combine and co-operate with that people from whom, for long
ages, you have stood apart, aliens and enemies to them, as they to
you. They count more in millions than you count in thousands. If
you desire that they and you should now join hands to carry the
boat over the rapids, it must be on terms which they will accept; on
terms of advantage to them as well as to you, – and the first
condition and very basis of a union must be the distinct acknow-
ledgment and assertion, in its widest extent, in its fullest force, power,
and plenitude, of the principle of ALLEGIANCE TO COUNTRY. On
any other basis no federation can form or be formed, take effect or
be of force, in Ireland now. To save mistake I ought to mention and
mark what it is I do *not* mean, as well as what my meaning is. I do
not mean that you should declare for Repeal. I scarcely know that
I can call myself a Repealer, farther than this – that I would not say
aye to the question if it were put to me to decide. The results of
Repeal would depend on the means and men by whom it should
have been accomplished. It might give to Ireland all that Ireland
wants, and is withering in want of, – equal liberty and equal laws,
science and art, manufacture and trade, respect and renown;
wealth to the merchant, security and comfort to the cottage, its
pride of place and power to the castle, fame and fortune to genius
and talent, all of that which ennobles and endears to man the land
he lives in; – this it might do. It might subject us to an odious and
ignoble tyranny. I am far from wishing you to take any course that
would pledge you to Repeal, or to any other political measure. I do
not write with a view to Repeal, or any other political object
whatever. My meaning is far more general, and states itself in
more general terms. Nothing is requisite or required that would
commit you, in particulars, to any political party, cause, or course
of conduct. But a full act and avowal of attachment and allegiance

to this island, in priority and preference to any and every other country, – this is required, and will be strictly required; not in mere idle form of protest and profession, but in full efficient proof and practice. That Ireland is your own mother-country, and her people your people, – that her interest and honor, her gain and her glory, are counted as your own, – that her rights and liberties you will defend, as part of your inheritance, – that in peace you will lead her progress, and carry her banner in battle, – that your labour shall be in her service, and your lives laid down at her need, – that henceforth you will be, not a foreign garrison but a national guard; – this you must declare and adopt, as the principle of your proceeding, and the spirit of your action, and the rule of your order; for these are the duties of nobility. Adopt this principle, and you are armed; on it is your safety and your strength; the future is fettered at your feet, and your name and race shall flourish and not fail. Ireland is yours for ages, yet on the condition that you will be Irishmen, in name, in faith, in fact. Refuse it, and you commit yourselves, in the position of paupers, to the mercy of English ministers and English members; you throw your very existence on English support, which England soon may find too costly to afford; you lie at the feet of events, you lie in the way of a people, and the movement of events and the march of a people shall be over you. Allegiance to this fair island; it is your title of tenure to the lands you hold, and in right of it you hold them. If you deny and disown it you assert another title, and must determine to hold your inheritance by force, at your own will and to our injury, in despite and defiance of us and ours for ever. This would be a bootless and feeble insult, and dangerous withal; for your title is worth little indeed under the law you would appeal to: that while from Ireland you take rank and revenue, blood and birth and name – everything that makes home, and binds to country – you yet look [not] to her, but to another land, for home and country; that you desert and disown, if not hate her old native people; that in England are your hearts and hopes, and that all your household-gods are English. This crime is charged to you; unjustly charged I trust it is – for a worse crime, and more infamous than disloyalty or treason to kings or crowns, is disloyalty or treason to country. It is a crime not made by lawyers, but made by God; a crime against nature itself – against all its laws, affections, interests, and instincts. Yet the charge is not made against you without colour of truth and show of reason. On every question that arises, in every contest and collision, whether of honor or interest, you take side and cause with England. All blame for this does not rest on you; but some of it does. Much and most of it rests on a class of men whose claim to attention, however strong, I must defer to a future letter. All such ground of charge must be removed and renounced. For ever, henceforth, the owners of our soil must be Irish. To all who own land or living in Ireland, Ireland henceforth must be the Queen-island. She holds in her hands the hostages for their fealty, and will not longer put up with TREASON. On no other common ground or general principle can a federation take place between the nobles of the land and the nation at large, than that of common faith and fealty to this their common country.

The formation of the Irish Party was hailed at the time by many as one step of a movement in the direction of Ireland. It may, perhaps, indicate a change of ideas, if not of feelings. You have probably begun to find out that if your feelings are English, yet your fortunes are Irish; that Ireland's peril is perilous to yourselves; that in renouncing your country, and adopting another, you renounce and revolt from the laws of nature; and that nature herself is strong enough to punish the treason. You have, moreover, got some slight cause to doubt whether England esteems your attachment as of any value, your interest as of much importance, or your very existence as worth the expense and peril of supporting. But we recognise nothing Irish in this party except is name; nothing that can entitle it to command or call round it the hearts or hopes of this people; or raise it to any higher position than that of a mere club, and a petty club, formed by a class for the single object of saving its own little interests from injury, at any cost to the country. Whether for its professed or its private objects, whether as an Irish party or as a landowners' club, it is equally and utterly inefficient, and can do nothing for the salvation of the country or for yours. It excludes the people. It embraces no great public principles, passions, purpose, or policy. It bears no banner, and shows no motto. It rallies no support, and inspires no confidence; proposes nothing, and promises nothing. To resist the minister, should his measures of relief or improvement be deemed injurious to the landowners, – this appears the sole object of the Irish Party. But your claims as landowners are no longer maintainable or defensible on their own merits and means. To maintain, you must connect them with those of your country. A union between parties of the same class, – a union of landowners with each other is adequate to no purpose now. The union required is a union between all classes of whom the people is composed. You are powerless without a people beside or behind you. You must call the commons into your council; and make their private interests and public objects, – nay, even perhaps their public passions, – a part of your policy. The Irish Party must expand and enlarge into the Irish people; or another, and more effective Association be framed.

To organise a new mode and condition of labour, – a new industrial system; to frame and fix a new order of society; in a word, to give to Ireland a new social constitution under which the natural capacity of this country would be put into effective action; the resources of its land, labour, and capital developed and made available; its slumbering and decaying energies of mind and muscle excited, directed, and employed; and the condition and character of its people reconstructed, improved, and elevated; – this I have already stated as the general object which now calls for the united action of the landowners and people of Ireland in association assembled. The energies of nature and action of time, working together in their wonted course and current, will indeed, in long or short, be adequate, without aid or effort of ours, to form a new and effective settlement of society; but the fabric thus formed will be raised out of the relics, and rest on the ruins, of the present existing people in all its classes. For their own safety and preservation it is necessary that all those classes should now combine to take the direction of that revolution which will otherwise effect itself, and which indeed is in actual process of being effected, without their consent, control, or guidance. That position has become too perilous to maintain. Your path of safety as well as of honor is now the public highway. No bye-way of your own will carry you through the perils that beset, and the greater perils that are before you. There are many and important questions at issue between you and the landholders, between you and the labourers, between you and the people at large, between you and other classes of the people, between those classes among themselves. No government, no legislation, no general statutes, no special statutes; no power on earth but the parties concerned; no mode on earth save that of voluntary agreement, can settle those questions. Why should we not meet, and settle them amicably? Leave them not to be settled by time, or to be settled by strength.

What! – to create a complete and efficient industrial economy; to form and give force to a new state and mode of existence; to organise and animate and put into healthy and vigorous action that complex living machine, a social system; to frame and adjust the fabric of society in its mightiest proportions and minutest parts, with all its vast and various interests, arrangements, orders, and conditions, independent yet involved, conflicting yet co-operating; –

what! to do all this? A work impossible to man; and which, in extent or detail, he never yet undertook or attempted to perform. A work of which the theory and principles are beyond his knowledge or discovery, and the practical execution beyond his utmost power. Nature has reserved it to herself, to effect by a process of her own; for which no artificial process ever was or can be substituted with success. A work we cannot do; God's hand alone, not man's, can do it. True, – and neither can you form in all its parts the smallest plant that grows. But sow the seed and the plant forms. The powers of vitality require but to be set in movement, and the contrivances of nature left free to act. Even so it is in the case we consider. That work may be done, and *you* must do it or others will; and you must do it at once, for it cannot be waited for. Nor is it, when examined, an undertaking that need dazzle or daunt by its magnitude or multiplicity the meanest mind of all among us. It includes no such complication of difficult questions as it may seem to do; and the only question actually involved is one easy of settlement when put in comparison with its apparent mass. Its theory contains itself in a single principle; its practical solution is comprised and completed in a single operation. Lay but the foundation and the work is done. Lay the foundation; nature effects the rest; society forms and fits itself – even as the plant grows when the seed is sown. Lay deep and strong, the only foundation that is firm under the foot of a nation – a secure and independent agricultural peasantry. A secure and independent agricultural peasantry is the only base on which a people ever rises, or ever can be raised; or on which a nation can safely rest. A productive and prosperous husbandry is the sole groundwork of a solid social economy. On it and out of it springs the mechanic, and artisan, and trading dealer; fed and fostered by it these swell into the manufacturer and merchant, who multiply into merchants and manufacturers; sustained by it still, these enlarge,

and gather, and solidify into companies, corporations, classes –
into great manufacturing and mercantile systems and interests,
which often, like unnatural children, disown and desert the
mother that bore and the nurse that fed them; without it there is
neither manufacture nor trade, nor means to make them, for it is
agriculture alone that furnishes those means. Food is our first
want – to procure it our first work. The agricultural class,
therefore, must precede and provide for every other. It is first in
order of nature, necessity, and time. It is an abundant agriculture
alone that creates and sustains manufactures, and arts, and traffic.
It is an increasing agriculture alone that extends them. For it is the
surplus of food it accumulates, after providing ordinary subsistence, that forms new wants and demands, and the modes and
means to meet and satisfy them. Such is the actual process; a
process that never yet was reversed, or carried out in any other
course or order; so it was at first, and so will it be for ever – in every
time, in every clime, in every country. Adopt this process; create
what has never yet existed in Ireland, an active and affluent
husbandry, a secure and independent agricultural peasantry, able
to accumulate as well as to produce; – do this, and you raise a
thriving and happy community, a solid social economy, a prosperous people, an effective nation. Create the husbandman, and you
create the mechanic, the artisan, the manufacturer, the merchant.
Thus you will work on the ordinance of God, in the order and with
the powers of nature. All the natural motives and means with
which man is endowed will come then to your relief and assistance,
and do the rest. Any further interference with the course and
process of natural laws would be useless and mischievous. Neither
monarchs nor mobs ever yet were able to manage or modify that
natural process with success; or ever attempted to enforce interference without doing grievous injury and gross injustice. The

abortive and mischievous legislation of both old and recent times affords lessons enough of this, if we choose to learn them.

There seems to be a vague impression on a large portion of the public mind of this country that national attention and exertion, as well as individual effort, should be directed into a course the reverse in its steps and stages of that natural order which I have pointed out. We are in the habit of hearing it asserted that a large development of manufacturing industry is what Ireland needs, and that to establish it should be her chief objects [*sic*]. It is even assumed, not unfrequently, that a manufacturing system must precede, and is the only mode of promoting, the improvement and prosperity of agriculture itself. This is an error I could wish to see abandoned. It distracts effort and attention from the point on which both ought to be directed, and on which they could act with effect. I am prepared to prove – what, indeed, any man may prove to himself – that neither by the private enterprise of individuals of companies, neither by the force of national feeling anyhow exerted, neither by public association or public action of any kind or extent, nor by government aid, if such aid could be expected, – neither by these or any other means and appliances can a manufacturing system be established in Ireland, nor so much as a factory built on firm ground, until the support of a numerous and efficient agricultural yeomanry be first secured. Good friends! you that are recommending us to encourage native manufacture and to form manufacturing associations; tradesmen and townsfolk of Ireland! will you cease to follow a phantom, and give hand and help to create such a yeomanry?

My general object, the formation of a new social economy, thus resolves itself into the formation of a new agricultural system. The principles on which that new system is to be founded must either be settled by agreement between the landowners and the people, or they must be settled by a struggle. What I think those principles ought to be, if they be made articles of agreement, as well as the practical mode of arriving at and arranging such agreement, I shall take another opportunity of stating.

You, however, my lords and gentlemen, it would appear from your present proceedings, have already settled among yourselves the entire future economy of your country – determined the fortunes and fate of this entire island – disposed of the existence of this little people of eight millions. The small landholdings are to be 'consolidated' into large farms, the small landholders 'converted' into 'independent labourers'; those labourers are, of course, to be paupers – those paupers to be supported by a poor law – that poor law is to be in your hands to manage and administer. Thus is to be got rid of the surplus of population beyond what the landowners require. Meantime, by forcible ejectments, forced surrender, and forced emigration, you are effecting the process of 'conversion' *a little* too rapidly, perhaps, for steady and safe working.

And so, it seems, you have doomed a people to extinction? And decreed to abolish Ireland? The undertaking is a large one. Are you sure your strength will bear you through it? Or are you sure your strength will not be tested? The settlement you have made requires nothing to give it efficacy, except the assent or acquiescence of eight millions of people. Will they assent or acquiesce? Will Ireland, at last, perish like a lamb, and let her blood sink in the ground, or will she turn as turns the baited lion? For my own part I can pronounce no opinion; and for you, my lords and gentlemen, if you have any doubts on the question, I think it would be wisdom to pause in your present course of proceeding until steps can be taken and measures adopted for effecting an accommodation and arrangement between you and the present occupiers of the soil, on terms that would preserve the rights and promote the interests of each party. If you persevere in enforcing a clearance of your lands you will force men to weigh your existence, as landowners, against the existence of an Irish people. The result of the struggle which that question might produce ought, at best, to be a matter of doubt in your minds; even though you should be aided, as you doubtless would be, by the unanimous and cordial support of the people of England, whose respect and esteem for you are so well known and so loudly attested.

I have the honor to remain, my lords and gentlemen, your humble and obedient servant.

JAMES F. LALOR

CHAPTER II

'The Nation', 15 May 1847
Tenants' Right and Landlords' Law

I may be told that this famine is a visitation of Divine Providence. But I do not admit that. I fear there is blasphemy in charging on the Almighty the result of our own doings. . . . God's famine is known by the general scarcity of food of which it is the consequence. There is no general scarcity. There has been no general scarcity in Ireland, either during the present or the last year, except in one solitary species of vegetable. The soil has produced its usual tribute for the support of those by whom it was cultivated . . . The vice inherent in our system of social and political economy is so settled that it eludes inquiry. You cannot trace it to the source. The poor man on whom the coroner holds an inquest has been murdered, but no one killed him. WHO DID IT? No one did it. Yet it was done. – RIGHT REVD DR HUGHES.

Tenakill, Abbeyleix, Saturday, May 8

I have just now seen in THE NATION of last Saturday, May 1, the foregoing extract from the lecture of Doctor Hughes, on the 'condition of Ireland'.

Doctor Hughes does not seem distinctly to understand how the failure of a single root can have produced a famine. The vice of our political and social economy is one that eludes inquiry. But is it, indeed, so obscure? Has it then been able to conceal or disguise itself? It must be dragged out. In self-defence the question is now forced on us, whether there be any particular class or institution specially chargeable? It is a question easily answered. Into the more remote causes of the famine it is needless now to inquire, but it is easily traced back to its immediate origin. The facts are few, and are soon told, and easily understood, when the conditions of [the] country it had to act on have first been stated. I state them from recollection. I have no returns at hand to refer to, but I shall be found generally correct.

There are in Ireland, or were last year, about 231,000 agricultural families, comprising 319,000 adult male labourers, depending altogether on wages for subsistence. If I commit any mistake, it is that of overstating the number of such families. There was not constant employment to be found for those 319,000 men, and the rate of wages was very low. The labourer, partially employed and poorly paid, was unable, on the mere hire of his hands, to feed himself and those who looked to him for food. He borrowed for six months (May 1 to Nov. 1) from some neighbouring farmer the use of a quarter of an acre of land. He paid for this six months' use the sum of £2. 12s. 6d. The farmer, however, manured the land; he manured it by paring off with the plough a thin layer of surface, which the labourer left to dry, made up into heaps, and burned into ashes, which he spread on the ground. On the land so manured – for in no other mode was it ever manured – he planted potatoes, and was able to live; and he *did* live on, from year to year, from youth to grey hair, and from father to son, in penury and patience. Whether the penury made the patience, or the patience made the penury, I stop not to inquire. Certain it is that they commonly go together. The details I am giving are sufficiently well known here, but I write for England. Such as I state him is, or was, the Irish labourer, that 'independent labourer', whose free and happy condition is now offered and recommended so strongly to the small landholder, as preferable to his own. Last year this man did as usual. He planted his potatoes; but when he came to dig them out, there were none to be digged. Two hundred and thirty thousand families began to die of hunger; and famine ran wild into fever.

The cultivated soil of Ireland is distributed, or was last year, into about 880,000 landholdings, each occupied by a family. Of this number of landholders, 510,000 were in occupation, each, of farms varying in size from one acre to ten, and none of them exceeding that extent. This class of men differed little in the appearance, but very much in the reality of circumstance and condition from the class of mere labourers. Their circumstances varied with the size of the holding; but the lowest among them stood far above the labourer. Their means of subsistence were somewhat greater, their securities for subsistence were far greater. They did not, as the labourers did, commonly starve or suffer grievous hunger through the summer months – the *famine months*, as we call them in this country. Those of them who held from five to ten acres of holding, enjoyed some little share of the comfort of life, which the careless and mirthful temperament of Ireland heightened into happiness. The men dressed well on Sunday, and the women gaily; at least in all parts of the country with which I am acquainted. The smallest landholders of this class were labourers also, – labourers with allotments, – labourers with assurance against positive starvation. Each man had at least a foot-hold of existence. Each man had potato-ground at least; at a high rent, indeed, but not so high as the con-acre rent. Still, however, the lowest grade of these men were miserable enough; but not so utterly so as the mere labourer. Their country had hope for them too, while she had none for the labourer. To avoid, if I can, confusion or complication of statement, I put out of view for the present the holdings of size beyond ten acres each, amounting in number to about 370,000. But such as I state it was the condition, so far as affects the small occupier I speak of, in which the famine found Ireland.

Two circumstances of this man's situation, and those not unimportant, remain yet, however, to be stated, in account for the past, and in calculation for the future. One of them is, that he held his land by no other assurance, legal or moral than his landlord's pecuniary personal interest in retaining him as tenant. He had commonly no lease of his holding; or, if he had, it was rendered null in effect by numberless circumstances which I cannot stop to state. The feelings that exist in England between landlord and tenant, coming down from old times, and handed as an heir-loom from generation to generation, – the feeling of family pride, the feeling of family attachment, the habit of the house, the fashion of the land, the custom of country, all those things that stand for laws, and are stronger than laws, – are here unknown; as indeed they are beginning to decay and die out in England. But the working farmer of Ireland, who held his own plough and acted as his own labourer, was able to pay a higher rent for his land than the farmer of any other class; and hence alone he continued to hold it. This was his title of tenure, – his only title; his security against the grazier and against the extensive tillage-farmer; his sole security for leave to live.

Such is the first circumstance requiring note. The second is this: The occupier I speak of, if his holding was very small, put the entire of it in tillage; if larger, he put a portion in pasture. In either case his tillage-ground was appropriated to two crops – a potato crop and a grain crop. He sowed grain for his landlord, he planted potatoes for himself. The corn paid the rent, the potato fed the tenant. When the holding was small, the grain crop was insufficient, alone, to balance rent; a portion of potatoes made up the deficiency by feeding a hog. When the holding was larger, the grain crop was often more than sufficient, with the help of a hog, to clear rent and tithe rent, county rate and poor rate. In such case the cultivator had a small overplus which he could actually dispose of as he liked; and he commonly laid it out in the purchase of mere luxuries, such as shoes, wearing apparel, and other articles of convenience. So stood the landholder of ten acres or under.

Last year this man did according to custom. He planted potatoes for his own support; he sowed corn for his landlord's rent. The potato perished; the landlord took the corn. The tenant cultivator paid his rents – was forced to pay them – sold his grain crop to pay them, and had to pray to man as well as to God for his daily bread. I state general facts; I stop not to count scattered and petty exceptions. Who is it says the landlords got no rent last year? Bernal Osborne says so;[1] and adds that the conduct of the Irish farmers in withholding their rents was most discreditable and disgraceful. One hundred voices and pens have said and repeated it. The landowners are in parliament and in the 'compositors' room'; the tenant cultivators are not. The lion is no painter. It may be so that in districts of Tipperary the tenants, or many of them, kept their corn for food – thus paying themselves for their labour, capital, and seed, and saving their own lives – instead of paying the land rent. It may be that in those districts the full rents were not paid; it may be that in parts of Galway, Mayo, Cork, and elsewhere, they *could not* be paid. The oat crop failed partially, as the potato failed wholly; and when these were the crops in the ground, the landowner, of course, in many cases lost a portion of his rent, as the tenant cultivator lost his entire provision of food. But these exceptions are inefficient against the fact I state. I say and assert that the landowners took entire possession of last year's harvest – of the whole effective sum and substance of that harvest. The food for this year's subsistence, the seed for next year's crop – the landlord took it all. He stood to his right and got his rent – and hunger was in five hundred thousand houses, pinching dearth in all, deadly famine in many. Famine, more or less, was in five hundred thousand families; famine, with all its diseases and decay; famine, with all its fears and horrors; famine, with all its dreadful pains and more dreadful debility. All pined and wasted, sickened and drooped; numbers died – the strong man, the fair maiden, the little infant; the landlord had got his rent.

Relief committees were formed and public works set on foot. The landowners grew bustling, if not busy, in the work of demanding relief and dispensing it. To the local relief funds very many of them, indeed, contributed nothing whatever; but there were others who contributed even so large a sum as 000.000 1/4 per cent on their annual income, and were most properly appreciated and praised as beneficent individuals; while several gave a per centage of double or thrice that amount – and Ireland rang with applause. They denounced the labour-rate act;[2] called for works which would increase the productive powers of the soil; and grew clamorous in the expression of pity for their suffering countrymen, whom they charged government with delivering up to famine by adopting an erroneous and inefficient system of relief. Finally, under the flag of their country they met in the Rotundo, and formed an 'Irish party' for the professed object of establishing and supporting an Irish policy for Irish purposes; that is to say, for the purpose of taking care that the pecuniary interests of the landowners of Ireland should suffer no detriment, more especially by any extension of poor law relief. Such is the history of the present famine. Does it furnish or suggest an answer to the concluding query of Dr Hughes?

But another famine is in preparation, and will surely come, no matter for fallacious statements of an increased breadth of tillage.

The lord of the soil had got his rent and become a public and professed patriot. The cultivator of the soil had lost his provision of food, and gone out to work on the public roads for public wages. The preparations for tillage, of course, were neglected. The tenant had neither seed nor subsistence; or if he had any small provision of either, he was soon deprived of it by the rules of the relief system. Whatever seed he might have saved from the landlord, whatever little means he possessed for making manure, whatever small capital was in his hands to work on with, were taken from him by relief committees and relieving officers. The law was laid down and acted on very generally, that no man should obtain either gratuitous relief or public employment until he should be first completely pauperised. If he had seed corn he should consume it, if he had a cow he should sell it -- and not a few of them said, as they are still saying, 'if he had land he should give it up'; otherwise he could have no title to relief. This was to say they chose rather to maintain wholly for ever after the first few months, than to maintain partially for those few months; rather to give permanent support than temporary aid; rather to create a pauper than to assist a struggling worker. This was to declare in favor of pauperism, and to vote for another famine. I am putting no blame on the parties to this proceeding. The reasons for it were plausible in appearance. I am merely stating a fact, and charging nothing more than mistake. 'We must guard against the evils', said the official authorities, 'of indiscriminate relief, and avoid the risk of pauperising the feelings of the peasantry, encouraging the spirit of dependence, and training them to the trade of beggars'. To me it seems it would have been safer to incur the risk of pauperising *their feelings* than the certainty of pauperising *their means*; and better even to take away *the will* to be independent than to take away *the power*. 'When there are such numbers utterly destitute', said the relief committee, 'why should we give a man relief who has a barrel of oats in his possession? it would be wasting silver and cheating *the poor*'. What was it to them that the barrel of oats, if kept for seed, would have produced 12 barrels at harvest? – a return of 1,200 per cent on the cost of feeding the man while consuming his poor little provision of corn seed.

The tenant was left without seed or subsistence. The effect is, that the smaller class of holdings remain uncropped and untilled, and in many cases abandoned. This class of holdings constituted a large portion of the tillage land of Ireland. The largest class of farms are exclusively under grass. The proportion of pasture diminishes as the farm grows smaller. The smallest class of holdings are exclusively in tillage; and these are not in the usual course of preparation for being cropped, but will, to all appearance of evidence, remain waste this year. The season is passing. The potato will not be planted to any efficient extent. No adequate substitute has been adopted or found – no adequate additional quantity of corn crop, or of any crop, has been sowed, or is in course of sowing. A famine for next year is all but secured. Numbers of the small occupiers have abandoned or surrendered their holdings. The landowners are assisting the natural operation of the famine instead of arresting it – putting the tenant out of his foot-hold of land instead of aiding him to retain and cultivate it. In every district the tenantry are being evicted in hundreds by legal process, by compelled surrenders, by forced sales for trifling sums – the price being very frequently paid by a receipt for fictitious or forgotten arrears. Those men are being converted into 'independent labourers'; and the number already evicted will form a considerable addition to a class too numerous even now for the demands or resources of the country – too many to be absorbed – too many to be supported. Another famine comes next year – a famine of undiminished powers of destruction to act on diminished powers of resource and resistance – a famine of equal vigour to act on weakened conditions. Additional numbers of the small occupiers are thrown out of occupation of land – the entire body I am speaking of are thrown out. It will not stop short of that, nor stop even there. Who can limit such an operation to ten-acre holdings, or limit it at all? They lose their land: they acquire, in lieu of it, that valuable species of Irish property, 'independent labour'. Stop one moment to look at the fact. Five hundred thousand families added to the two hundred and thirty thousand who form the present mass of labour – 670,000 adult males converted into 'independent labourers' – 670,000 hands added to those 319,000 already so successfully engaged in independent labour. But surely I overstate. No one will believe this can happen until it has actually happened. No one believes in the future – no one sees tomorrow as he sees to-day. I may not be correct to the very last figure, but I am effectively correct. But is it I that say this result will come – is it I alone? Every speaker in parliament whose words carry weight forestates this result – defends, justifies, urges it; and not a voice rises to protest against the principle, the feasibility, the consequences. It is the policy and purpose of every act that is passing through the legislature. 'Whereas, it is desirable that the conversion of the inferior classes of Irish landholders into independent labourers shall take effect as speedily and safely as possible, and without serious damage or danger to the English interest or the English garrison in Ireland' – I read this as the preamble of every Irish act of the session. It is assumed and set down that such conversion is to take place – not partially neither, but universally. No authority assumes, no argument asserts, that the small occupiers are *too many*, and ought to be reduced. The assertion is that the small occupier is a man who ought not to be *existing*. He ought to be, and is to be henceforth, an independent labourer. No cause, moreover, is operating against one of the class that is not operating against all.

But the confiscation will not be limited to ten-acre holdings. There are causes in operation which will shortly render it impossible for tillage-land to pay as high a rent as land under grass. Many causes – some natural, others artificial – render it impossible to produce corn in this country at so low a cost, quality for quality, as it can be produced in most others. Our corn will soon be undersold in the market by a superior article – a result rendered surer and speedier by the present increased demand for foreign corn. Shortly, too, the house-feeding of cattle can no longer be carried on. Even if the repeal of the corn-duty should realise the utmost expectations of its advocates, and if there should be, consequently, a proportionate increase in the demand for beef, mutton, butter, and wool, yet the tillage land of Ireland, turned into grass land, will be fully adequate to supply that increased demand. House-feeding will be unable to compete against grass-feeding, or to pay for itself. Together with corn, therefore, the root-crops will no longer be raised. A regular system of active cultivation is sustained and supported by corn alone. The agriculture that employs and maintains millions will leave the land, and an agriculture that employs only thousands will take its place. Ireland will become a pasture ground once again, as it was before, and its agricultural population of tillage farmers and labourers will decay and die out by degrees, or vanish and become extinct at once; even as heretofore, from the same cause, in many times and countries, populations as numerous, melting away by a rapid mortality, or mouldering out by slow but sure decay, have perished and passed away from the earth; for classes of people, nor entire populations, nor nations themselves, are not fixed or immortal, any more than the individual men that compose them.

The eight thousand individuals who are absolute owners of Ireland by divine right and the grant of God, confirmed (*by themselves*) in sundry successive acts of parliament, have a full view of all those coming results I have stated, and have distinctly declared their intention of serving notice to quit on the people of Ireland. Bernal Osborne asserts that the small landholders[3] are unable (*after having paid their rents*) to support themselves out of the land; and that they must be completely got rid of. The landowners have adopted the process of depopulating the island and are pressing it forward to their own destruction or to ours. They are declaring that they and we can no longer live together in this land. They are enforcing self-defence on us. They are, at least, forcing on us the question of submission or resistance; and I, for one, shall give my vote for resistance.

Before I examine that question, and state what I conceive to be the true grounds, limits, and mode of resistance, I propose making one other and last appeal to the landowners to adopt the only course that can now save a struggle.

JAMES F. LALOR

CHAPTER III

'The Nation', 5 June 1847
A National Council

TO THE EDITOR OF THE NATION

Tenakill, Abbeyleix, Tuesday, May 25

SIR – In the leading article of last Saturday's NATION it is stated that the 'Reproductive Committee' has changed its name, enlarged its basis, and constituted itself into what the writer would seem desirous to consider to be the nucleus of a 'National Council'.[4] He seems also to attach an importance to the transaction, of which, I fear, it is wholly undeserving.

THE NATION gives no report, and I have seen none elsewhere, of the proceedings of the meeting at which the alleged alterations were made. I know nothing, therefore, of the name, nature, principles, or purpose of the new association into which the committee has resolved itself. I write consequently in ignorance, and on mere supposition.

But I know that of necessity it will consist, effectively, if not avowedly, of landowners only. Its composition and character will be determined and limited as strictly by circumstances as they could by formal rule of constitution. Originating in Dublin, without any virtual constituency throughout the country to empower or support, formed by its own private act, not by public action, it will never, in public estimation, be anything more than an association of landowners; and it will be practical wisdom to attempt no revolt against a public decision, and to assume no other character or functions than those which general opinion will have certainly assigned to it. Should it be able to establish and extend itself, a few individuals from other classes might doubtless be induced to join it – a few mercantile and professional men, tradesmen, and tenant-farmers; but never in sufficient number to enable it to assume the character or exercise the functions of a National Council. Let it profess to be, what in fact it is, an association of landed proprietors, and pretend to be nothing more. This will be its true and most effective policy.

But no association of landowners, acting alone, can settle a single question of all those which are now fermenting in every house and every heart throughout the island. Be its objects what they may, the noblest or meanest, the greatest or pettiest, not one of them can be effected without the assent and aid of those who occupy the soil and inhabit the land, and who will continue to be occupiers and inhabitants in despite and defiance of open force or covert fraud, of avowed enemies or hollow friends.

If its founders, however, be honest, earnest, and capable, and should they succeed in obtaining the adhesion of any considerable number of the landed proprietors, the nascent association may be made to form one component part of a National Council, of which the Commons of Ireland – tenant-farmers and trading classes – would constitute the other portion.

As the most ready and feasible mode that occurs to me of organising such Council, I beg to present, for consideration and correction, the hasty draft of plan which is stated in the following suggestions: –

1. That the 'Reproductive Committee' do immediately constitute itself into an association of landowners, to be composed exclusively of Irish landed proprietors.

2. That should such proposed association of landowners become too numerous to act as a deliberative assembly, it shall appoint a managing committee of one or two hundred members, empowered and instructed to assume the office of standing, and speaking, and acting, as the accredited organ of the landed proprietors of Ireland.

3. That a tenant-league, or association of tenant-farmers be formed with as little delay as possible in each of the several counties of Ireland.

4. That every such county league of tenant-farmers shall appoint a managing committee of not less than *five*, nor more than *twelve* members – the number to be fixed according to the extent and population of the county.

5. That a trade society, for the revival and promotion of Irish manufacture, be established in each of the thirty most populous cities and towns of the kingdom.

6. That every such trade society shall appoint a secretary, or a president and secretary, or a managing committee of from three to eight members, according to the greater or smaller population of the town or city.

7. That those tenant-league committees, trade committees, and trade officers, either under special powers and instructions to that effect, if allowed by the convention act,[5] or otherwise, through the concurrence of accidental circumstances or other perfectly legal and moral contrivance, shall assemble together in Dublin, to consult and determine upon such questions affecting the interests of the tenant-farmers and trading classes of Ireland as may be brought before them; and shall, further, be empowered

(or permitted) to treat, confer, and enter into agreement with the landowners' association on all those several questions.

8. That those committees be further vested with full powers (or allowed full permission) to hold such conference with the landed proprietors, in whatever mode may be found most eligible and convenient; and to make such agreement as aforesaid, in whatever form may be deemed most conclusive and satisfactory, and on such guarantees and securities as may be considered sufficient.

This is a very hurried and imperfect sketch of my ideas on the mode in which I think a National Council might be constituted, such as the people of Ireland would acknowledge and accept in that character. The primary proceeding of forming the several tenant-leagues and trade-societies is the only essential portion of the plan. There are many modes in which the ulterior proceedings might be conducted without violating the convention act. If the society formed by the Reproductive Committee recommend and carry out this proceeding, or some analogous proceeding, they will have deserved well of their country, saved and strengthened their own class, and done a deed in history.

JAMES F. LALOR

CHAPTER IV

'Tipperary Vindicator', 24 July 1847
Tenant League – Meeting of Tipperary

TO THE EDITOR OF THE TIPPERARY VINDICATOR

SIR – A brief statement of the circumstances which appear to require and justify a defensive movement on the part of the tenant-farmers, may possibly be thought desirable.

The mode in which the lands of this country have hitherto been let to the occupying tenant, was one which neither gave him nor recognised any right of property or possession in the soil which he cultivates, but on the contrary refused and repudiated any such right. Complete insecurity of property to the actual tiller of the soil was the principle and rule acted on. A state of helpless and hopeless poverty, of tyranny and terror such as never prevailed in any other civilised country, imperfect cultivation, scanty production, a miserable people, no capital to create manufactures, no means to consume and support them effectively – these were the natural and inevitable results. Last year this state of things came at length to a destructive and desolating famine, such as Europe has not witnessed for ages.

In no other country could the failure of a single root have produced a famine. The mode in which it did so in Ireland is soon stated and easily understood. A single sentence states cause and effect. The tenure and terms on which the small occupier held his land obliged him to depend altogether on the potatoes for food; rent, and tax, and other demands took the whole of his corn crop. The potato failed last year; the landlord took the corn – the tenant famished. In the parish I reside in several families paid up their rents to the last penny at November, and died of hunger during the winter.

Last year the potato produced about one-fourth of an average crop – subsistence for three months instead of for twelve. This year, on the highest estimate, about one-tenth of an average crop has been planted, taking Ireland throughout – subsistence for five weeks instead of fifty-two. The landlord will demand his rent, as he did last year; nor famine nor fever can fright him, for the law stands beside him – the law he made himself. Once again the tenant will be destitute, and must turn beggar at the door of the poor-house. But does he hold more than 25 perches (Irish) of land? He must surrender his holding before he can receive relief. He refuses to surrender it, and dies of hunger; – he consents to surrender it, and becomes a pauper for life.

Meanwhile, the landlords have determined and declared that the whole and entire body of the working tillage farmers of Ireland must be completely rooted out and got rid of – that they ought never to have existed and must now cease to exist. Throughout Ireland, putting Ulster aside, the mass of the small occupiers are under actual process of ejectment, or have been served with notice to quit.

To protect this class of our people, to preserve them to the cause and to the hopes of their country, to secure and elevate them for the time to come, to assert and establish for the tenant-farmers and for the people of this island the right that belongs to them – their right of existence, their right of full and honest subsistence, their right of property, their right of security – their right, in a word, of living as God and nature meant and made them to live, by their own labour, on their own land, in this their own country – not as prisoned slaves in a workhouse, or as wretched paupers in a public gang – such are the general objects of the proposed meeting and association. Those who approve of them will of course subscribe the requisition, procure as many signatures as possible, and use all the means in their power to cause the attendance at the meeting of the entire population of their several districts.

It will not, I should hope, be used as an argument against the proposed County Association that Tipperary appears to stand less in need, for the present at least, of such an association than most other counties. True, Tipperary suffered less by the fame [*sic*] of last year, and is suffering less from eviction during the present, than any other county of the Catholic provinces, excepting Wexford and Wicklow; but this present immunity is merely temporary, and is a reason for immediate action instead of against it. Ireland will be stricken down in divisions, as the bundle of rods was broken; and we belong not to Tipperary but to Ireland.

JAMES F. LALOR

CHAPTER V

'The Irish Felon', 24 June 1848
Mr Lalor's Letter to the Editor of the 'Irish Felon'

DEAR SIR, – In assenting to aid in the formation and conduct of a journal intended to fill the place and take up the mission of THE UNITED IRISHMAN, I think it desirable to make a short statement of the principles and conditions, public and personal, on which alone I would desire to be accepted as a partner in this undertaking. I think there is none of them to which you will object or demur, and that I may already consider them as articles of agreement. There are some of them which may possibly strike you at first as admitting question, or requiring to be qualified; but I am convinced you will find our views to be essentially the same, although perhaps put into a different dialect and a different form of expression.

And in the first place, and prior to everything else, I feel bound to state that I join you on the clear understanding that I am engaging, not in a mercantile concern, nor in any private specu-lation or enterprise whatever, but in a political confederacy for a great public purpose. Money must not be admitted among our objects or motives; and no money must be made by those, or any of those, concerned in the conduct of this journal. You, and I, and each, and all of us, must determine to leave this office as poor as we entered it. This condition is more important than may appear on first view; and I believe it absolutely requisite to make and insist on it as a principle of action. You may not, and indeed cannot, be aware of all its necessity, nor of many of the motives and grounds on which I desire to have it entered as an article of agreement between ourselves, and between us and the public. In a letter intended for publication (if you see fit), I do not for the present think proper to give any full statement; but in private I feel assured that I shall be able to satisfy your mind on this matter.

To establish an ordinary newspaper on the common motive of vesting a capital to advantage is, doubtless, quite legitimate. But to found such a journal as 'THE FELON', on the views which you and I entertain, for the mere purpose, in whole or in part, of making a fortune or making a farthing, would be a felon's crime indeed, deserving no hero's doom, lamented death, or honoured exile, but death on the scaffold, amid the scoff and scorn of the world. For years we have seen men in Ireland alternately trading on the government and trading on the country, and making money by both; and you do not imagine, perhaps, to what a degree the public mind has been affected with a feeling of suspicion by the circumstance – a feeling deepened, extended, and justified, by all we see or know of ourselves. For, indeed, the craving to get money – the niggard reluctance to give money – the coward fear of losing or laying out money – is the bad and coarse point that is most apparent in the character of all ranks and classes of our people; and I often fear it argues an utter absence of all heroism from our national temperament, and of all the romantic passions, whether public or private. In other countries men marry for love; in Ireland they marry for money. Elsewhere they serve their country for their country's thanks or their country's tears, – here they do it for their country's money. At this very time, when Ireland, to all appearance, is stripping for her last struggle on this side of ages, there are, I am convinced, many persons among the middle classes who refuse to

fall into the national march, or countenance the national movement, merely from the hope – in most cases as vain as it is vile – of
obtaining some petty government place; or from the fear of losing
some beggarly employment or emolument; and I know myself in
this county many and many a sturdy and comfortable farmer who
refuses to furnish himself with a pike, merely and solely because it
would cost him two shillings. For ourselves – I say nothing of
others – let us aim at higher and better rewards than mere money-
rewards. Better and higher rewards has Ireland in her hands. If we
succeed, we shall obtain these; and if we do not succeed, we shall
deserve none. In cases like this, the greatest crime that man can
commit is the crime of failure. I am convinced it has become
essential to our own fame and our effectiveness – to the success of
our cause and the character of our country, to keep clear and
secure ourselves from the suspicion, that our only object may
be nothing more than a long and lucrative agitation. The
Confederation pledged its members to accept no office or place of
profit from an English government. That pledge was efficient,
perhaps, for its own professed purpose, but not for others, – for an
'agitation' has places and profits of its own to bestow. Let them say
of us whatever else they will – let them call us felons, and treat us
as such, but let them not at least have the power to call us swindlers. We may never be famous: let us not become infamous. For the
Proprietors of this Paper, let their capital be replaced, but nothing
more. For the conductors and contributors, let their entire expenses
be defrayed, and defrayed, if you will, on the most liberal estimate,
but nothing more. If any surplus remain, large or little, it is
required in support and aid of our general objects, and to that
purpose I am clearly of opinion it ought to be devoted. It is perfectly
plain to me that a newspaper of itself cannot achieve those objects,
any more than a battery can carry a camp or a fortress. A public
journal is, indeed, indispensable; but it is chiefly in order to cover

and protect other operations, and those operations must be paid for. They will not pay for themselves. A public fund is wanted, – a large one is wanted, – it is wanted immediately; and we have no present mode of forming one, except by throwing into it the whole surplus profits of THE FELON.

But some of us may have families – we may perish in this enterprise – and what of them? Leave them to God and to Ireland; or, if you fear to trust either, then stay at home, and let others do the work.

For these, and other still more important reasons, needless to be stated as yet, I certainly could have wished that this journal had been established on a subscribed capital, and the effective owner-ship vested in a joint-stock company of, say eight hundred or a thousand proprietors. What is there to hinder that this arrangement should be made even now? It would contain securities, and create powers, which no other could offer or pretend to. There are, indeed, some practical difficulties in the way; but they might easily, I think, be overcome. Whether any such arrangement be adopted or not, I believe, however, that I am fully warranted in desiring – and I think our own true interest and honour concur in demanding – that the FELON office shall not be a commercial establishment, but organised and animated as a great political association. And, for my own part, I enter it with the hope and determination to make it an armed post, a fortress for freedom to be, perhaps, taken and re-taken again, and yet again; but never to surrender, nor stoop its flag, till that flag shall float above a liberated nation.

Without agreement as to our objects we cannot agree on the course we should follow. It is requisite the paper should have but one purpose; and the public should understand what that purpose is. Mine is not to repeal the Union, nor restore Eighty-two. This is not the year '82; this is the year '48. For Repeal I never went into 'Agitation' and will not go into insurrection. On that question I refuse to arm, or to act in any mode; and the country refuses. O'Connell made no mistake when he pronounced it not worth the price of one drop of blood; and for myself, I regret it was not left in the hands of Conciliation Hall, whose lawful property it was and is.[6] Moral force and Repeal, the means and the purpose, were just fitted to each other, – *Arcades ambo*, balmy Arcadians both. When the means were limited, it was only proper and necessary to limit the purpose. When the means were enlarged, the purpose ought to have been enlarged also. Repeal, in its vulgar meaning, I look on as utterly impracticable by any mode of action whatever; and the constitution of '82 as absurd, worthless, and worse than worthless. The English government will never concede or surrender it to any species of moral force whatsoever; and the country-peasantry will never arm and fight for it, – neither will I. If I am to stake life and fame it must assuredly be for something better and greater; more likely to last, more likely to succeed, and better worth success. And a stronger passion, a higher purpose, a nobler and more needful enterprise is fermenting in the hearts of the people. A mightier question moves Ireland to-day than that of merely repealing the Act of Union. Not the constitution that Tone died to abolish, but the constitution that Tone died to obtain – independence, full and absolute independence, for this island, and for every man within this island. Into no movement that would leave an enemy's garrison in possession of all our lands, masters of our liberties, our lives, and all our means of life and happiness – into no such move-ment will a single man of the greycoats enter with an armed hand, whatever the town population may do. On a wider fighting-field, with stronger positions and greater resources than are afforded by the paltry question of Repeal, must we close for our final struggle with England, or sink and surrender. Ireland her own, – Ireland her own, and all therein, from the sod to the sky. The soil of Ireland for the people of Ireland, to have and to hold from God alone who gave it – to have and to hold to them and their heirs for ever, without suit or service, faith or fealty, rent or render, to any power under Heaven. From a worse bondage than the bondage of any foreign government, – from a dominion more grievous and grinding than the dominion of England in its worst days, – from the cruellest tyranny that ever yet held its vulture clutch on the body and soul of a country, – from the robber rights and robber rule that have turned us into slaves and beggars in the land which God gave us for ours, – Deliverance, oh Lord, Deliverance or Death, – Deliverance, or this island a desert. This is the one prayer, and terrible need, and real passion of Ireland to-day, as it has been for ages. Now, at last, it begins to shape into defined and desperate purpose; and into it all meaner and smaller purposes must settle and merge. It might have been kept in abeyance, and away from the sight of the sun – aye, even till this old native race had been finally conquered out and extinguished, *sub silentio*, without noise or notice. But once propounded and proclaimed as a principle, not in the dusk of remote country districts, but loudly and proudly, in the tribunes of the capital, it must now be accepted and declared as the first and main Article of Association in the National Covenant of organised defence and armed resistance; as the principle to take ground, and stand, and fight upon. When a greater and more ennobling enterprise is on foot, every inferior and feebler project or proceeding will soon be left in the hands of old women, of dastards, impostors, swindlers, and imbeciles. All the strength and manhood of the island, – all the courage, energies, and ambition, – all the passions, heroism, and chivalry, – all the strong men and all the strong minds, – all those things that make revolutions, will quickly desert it, and throw themselves into the greater movement, throng into the larger and loftier undertaking, and flock round the banner that flies nearest to the sky. There go the young, the gallant, the gifted, and the daring; and there, too, go the wise. For wisdom knows that in national action *littleness* is more fatal than the wildest rashness; that greatness of object is essential to greatness of effort, strength, and success; that a revolution ought never to take its stand on low or narrow ground, but seize on the broadest and highest ground it can lay hands on; and that a petty enterprise seldom succeeds. Had America aimed or declared for less than independence, she would, probably, have failed, and been a fettered slave to-day.

Not to repeal the Union, then, but to repeal the conquest, – not to disturb or dismantle the empire, but to abolish it utterly for ever, – not to fall back on '82 but act up to '48, – not to resume or restore an old constitution, but to found a new nation, and raise up a free people, and strong as well as free, and secure as well as strong, based on a peasantry rooted like rocks in the soil of the land, – this is my object, as I hope it is yours; and this, you may be assured, is the easier, as it is the nobler and the more pressing enterprise. For Repeal, all the moral means at our disposal have in turns been used, abused, and abandoned. All the military means it can command will fail as utterly. Compare the two questions. Repeal would require a national organisation; a central representative authority, formally convened, formally elected; a regular army, a regulated war of concerted action and combined movement. When shall we have them? Where is your National Council of Three Hundred? Where is your National Guard of Three Hundred Thousand?[7] On Repeal, Ireland, of necessity, should resolve and act *by the kingdom*, all together, linked and led; and if beaten in the kingdom, there would be nothing to fall back upon. She could not possibly act by parishes. To club and arm would not be enough, or, rather, it would be nothing; and for Repeal alone Ireland will neither club nor arm. The towns only will do so. A Repeal-war would probably be the fight and defeat of a single field-day; or, if protracted, it would be a mere game of chess – and England, be assured, would beat you in a game of chess. On the other question all circumstances differ, as I could easily show you. But I have gone into this portion of the subject prematurely and unawares, and here I stop – being reluctant, besides, to trespass too long on the time of her Majesty's legal and military advisers.

I would regret much to have my meaning, in any degree, misconceived. I do not desire, by any means, to depreciate the value and importance of Repeal, in the valid and vigorous sense of the term, but only in its vulgar acceptation. I do not want to make the tenure-question the sole or main topic and purpose of THE FELON, or to make Repeal only secondary and subservient. I do not wish – far from it – to consider the two questions as antagonistic or distinct. My wish is, to combine and cement the two into one; and so perfect, and reinforce, and strengthen both, and carry both. I, too, want to bring about an alliance and 'combination of classes' – an alliance more wanted and better worth, more feasible, effective, and honourable, than any treasonable alliance with the enemy's garrison, based on the surrender and sacrifice of the rights and lives of the Irish people. I want to ally the town and the country. Repeal is the question of the town population; the land tenure question is that of the country peasantry; both combined, taking each in its full extent and efficacy, form the question of Ireland – her question for the battle day.

The principle I state, and mean to stand upon, is this, that the entire ownership of Ireland, moral and material, up to the sun, and down to the centre, is vested of right in the people of Ireland; that they, and none but they, are the land-owners and law-makers of this island; that all laws are null and void not made by them, and all titles to land invalid not conferred or confirmed by them; and that this full right of ownership may and ought to be asserted and enforced by any and all means which God has put in the power of man. In other, if not plainer, words, I hold and maintain that the

entire soil of a country belongs of right to the entire people of that
country, and is the rightful property, not of any one class, but of
the nation at large, in full effective possession, to let to whom they
will, on whatever tenures, terms, rents, services, and conditions
they will; one condition being, however, unavoidable and essential,
the condition that the tenant shall bear full, true, and undivided
fealty and allegiance to the nation, and the laws of the nation,
whose land he holds, and own no allegiance whatsoever to any
other prince, power, or people, or any obligation of obedience or
respect to their will, orders, or laws. I hold further, and firmly
believe, that the enjoyment by the people of this right of first
ownership in the soil, is essential to the vigour and vitality of all
other rights; to their validity, efficacy, and value; to their secure
possession, and safe exercise. For let no people deceive themselves,
or be deceived by the words, and colours, and phrases, and forms
of a mock freedom, by constitutions, and charters, and articles,
and franchises. These things are paper and parchment, waste and
worthless. Let laws and institutions say what they will, this fact
will be stronger than all laws, and prevail against them, – the fact
that those who own your lands will make your laws, and command
your liberties and your lives. But this is tyranny and slavery;
tyranny in its widest scope, and worst shape; slavery of body and
soul, from the cradle to the coffin – slavery, with all its horrors, and
with none of its physical comforts and security; even as it is in
Ireland, where the whole community is made up of tyrants, slaves,
and slave-drivers. A people whose lands and lives are thus in the
keeping and custody of others, instead of in their own, are not in a
position of common safety. The Irish famine of '46 is example and
proof. The corn crops were sufficient to feed the island. But the
landlords *would* have their rents, in spite of famine, and defiance of
fever. They took the whole harvest, and left hunger to those who
raised it. Had the people of Ireland been the landlords of Ireland,

not a human creature would have died of hunger, nor the failure of the potato been considered a matter of any consequence.

This principle, then, – that the property and possession of the land, as well as the powers of legislation, belong of right to the people who live in the land and under the law, – do you assent to it in its full integrity, and to the present and pressing necessity of enforcing it? Your *reason* may assent, yet your *feelings* refuse and revolt, – or those of others at least may do so. Mercy is for the merciful; and you may think it pity to oust and abolish the present noble race of land-owners, who have ever been so pitiful and compassionate themselves. What! is your sympathy for a class so great, and your sympathy for a whole people so small[?]. For those same land-owners are now treading out the very life and existence of an entire people, and trampling down the liberties and hopes of this island for ever. It is a mere question between a people and a class, – between a people of eight millions and a class of eight thousand. They or we must quit this island. It is a people to be saved or lost; – it is the island to be kept or surrendered. They have served us with a general writ of ejectment. Wherefore I say, let them get a notice to quit at once; or we shall oust possession under the law of nature. There are men who claim protection for them, and for all their tyrannous rights and powers, being 'as one class of the Irish people'. I deny the claim. They form no class of the Irish people, or of any other people. Strangers they are in this land they call theirs, – strangers here and strangers everywhere; owning no country and owned by none; rejecting Ireland and rejected by England; tyrants to this island and slaves to another; here they stand, hating and hated, – their hand ever against us as ours against them, an outcast and ruffianly horde, alone in the world and alone in its history, a class by themselves. They do not now, and never did, belong to this island at all. Tyrants and traitors have they ever been to us and ours since first they set foot on our soil. Their crime it is, and not England's, that Ireland stands where she does to-day, – or rather it is our own, that have borne them so long. Were they a class of the Irish people the Union could be repealed without a life lost. Had they been a class of the Irish people that Union would have never been. But for them we would now be free, prosperous, and happy. Until they be removed no people can ever take root, grow up, and flourish here. The question between them and us must, sooner or later, have been brought to a deadly issue. For heaven's sake and Ireland's let us settle it now, and not leave it to our children to settle. Indeed, it *must* be settled now; – for it is plain to any ordinary sight that they or we are doomed. A cry has gone up to heaven for the living and for the dead, – to save the living, to avenge the dead.

There are, however, many landlords, perhaps, and certainly a few, not fairly chargeable with the crimes of their order; and you may think it hard they should lose their lands. But recollect [that] the principle I assert would make Ireland, *in fact* as she is *of right*, mistress and queen of all those lands; that she, poor lady, had ever a soft heart and grateful disposition; and that she may, if she please, in reward of allegiance, confer new titles or confirm the old. Let us crown her a queen: and then – let her do with her lands as a queen may do.

In the case of any existing interest, of what nature soever, I feel assured that no question but one would need to be answered. Does the owner of that interest assent to swear allegiance to the people of Ireland, and to hold in fee from the Irish nation? If he assent he may be assured he will suffer no loss. No eventual or permanent loss I mean; for some temporary loss he must assuredly suffer. But such loss would be incidental and inevitable to any armed insurrection whatever, no matter on what principle the right of resistance should be resorted to. If he refuse, then I say – away with him – out of this land with him – himself and all his robber rights, and all the things himself and his rights have brought into our island – blood, and tears, and famine, and the fever that goes with famine.

Between the relative merits and importance of the two rights, the people's right to the land, and their right to legislation, I do not mean or wish to institute any comparison. I am far, indeed, from desirous to put the two rights in competition or contrast, for I consider each alike as the natural complement of the other, necessary to its theoretical completeness and practical efficacy. But, considering them for a moment as distinct, I do mean to assert this, – that the land question contains, and the legislative question does *not* contain, the materials from which victory is manufactured; and that, therefore, if we be truly in earnest, and determined on success, it is on the former question, and not on the latter, we must take our stand, fling out our banner, and hurl down to England our gage of battle. Victory follows that banner alone – that, and no other. This island is ours, and have it we will, if the leaders be but true to the people, and the people be true to themselves.

The rights of property may be pleaded. No one has a higher respect for the real rights of property than I have; but I do not class among them the robber's right, by which the lands of this country are now held in fee from the British crown. I acknowledge no right of property in a small class, which goes to abrogate the rights of a numerous people. I acknowledge no right of property in eight thousand persons, be they noble or ignoble, which takes away all rights of property, security, independence, and existence itself, from a population of eight millions, and stands in bar to all the political rights of the island, and all the social rights of its inhabitants. I acknowledge no right of property which takes the food of millions, and gives them a famine – which denies to the peasant the right of a home, and concedes, in exchange, the right of a workhouse. I deny and challenge all such rights, howsoever founded or enforced. I challenge them, as founded only on the code of the brigand, and enforced only by the sanction of the hangman. Against them I assert the true and indefeasible right of property – the right of our people to live in this land, and possess it, – to live in it in comfort, security, and independence, and to live in it by their own labour, on their own land, as God and nature meant them to do. Against them I shall array, if I can, all the forces that yet remain in this island. And against them I am determined to make war, – to their destruction, or my own.

These are my principles and views. I shall have other opportunities to develope and defend them. I have some few other requisitions to make; but I choose to defer them for other reasons besides want of time and space. Our first business, before we can advance a step, is to fix our own footing and make good our position. That once done, this contest must, if possible, be brought to a speedy close.

JAMES F. LALOR
Tenakill, Abbeyleix, 21st June, 1848.

CHAPTER VI

'The Irish Felon', 1 July 1848
The First Step – The Felon Club

THE FELON has not been established for the mere purpose of speculating, or theorising, or teaching, but for that of acting, too. We feel the fact, that it was the absence of any thing like effective action that has made every Irish movement hitherto a ridiculous, as well as melancholy, failure, – a matter of mirth to our enemies, and of mockery to every people but ourselves.

A meeting that spreads over miles, – an association that covers the island, – a movement that continues through years, – may each alike be just as much a mere speculator, theorist, and talker, as any one individual man. And such has been the Irish Repeal movement up to this day. What was Conciliation Hall? What was Tara?[8] A million of men stood there. What did they do? Speculated, spouted, cheered, resolved, declared, petitioned, and adjourned.

We have resolved, therefore, not alone to advise others to act but to assist them to the utmost measure of our means, and the best of our ability; and to adopt ourselves the most extensive and vigorous action which public support will enable us to take and maintain.

The amount of support which we could rely on as effective must be tendered us on a clear statement and full view of our principles, objects, and intended course of proceedings. All support otherwise obtained would, in effect, be obtained under false pretences; would be altogether unsound and fictitious; and would fail us when resorted to. We will not voluntarily deceive the public in the smallest particular, and we earnestly hope that no portion of the public will say or do aught that would tend to deceive us. We fear that popular meetings in Ireland have not unfrequently applauded sentiments and voted resolutions over night which they were utterly unprepared to act upon in the morning. But no people have a right to cheer men on to the foot of the breach, or the foot of the scaffold, and then desert them. Neither, on the other hand, ought any man leave the great mass and general mind of the country too far behind him. The very foremost banner should never be too far forward. In advance, but not miles nor months in advance, – a stride before his regiment, a day before the people – this is a leader's place.

We hold the present existing government of this island, and all existing rights of property in our soil, to be mere usurpation and tyranny, and to be null and void, as of moral effect; and our purpose is to abolish them utterly, or lose our lives in the attempt. The right founded on conquest, and affirmed by laws made by the conquerors themselves, we regard as no other than the right of the robber on a larger scale. We owe no obedience to laws enacted by another nation without our assent; nor respect to assumed rights of property which are starving and exterminating our people. The present salvation and future security of this country require that the English government should at once be abolished, and the English garrison of landlords instantly expelled. Necessity demands it, – the great necessity of self-defence. Self-defence – self-protection – it is the first law of nature, and the first duty of man. We refuse all appeal to the English Parliament to abolish itself. We will not appeal against the robber to the robber's den, nor against the landlord to a Parliament of landlords. We advise the people to organise and arm at once in their own defence. We mean to assist them; and to set example by organising and arming ourselves.

Such is a brief statement in outline of our principles and purposes. It leaves the principles undefended, the purposes undeveloped, all objections unanswered, all details unexplained, – and details are frequently as important as principle or purpose; but these omissions are matter of mere necessity for the present.

It remains to state our intended course of proceeding, so far as may be necessary and expedient.

We have determined to set about creating, as speedily as possible, a military organisation, of which the FELON Office shall be the centre and citadel.

As our first step of proceeding, we are now founding a club which it is intended shall consist of one, two, or more persons from each parish throughout Ireland, who are to be in immediate connexion and correspondence with this Office.

The number of members is not intended to be limited by any positive rule. But every person is not to be admissible. Certain qualifications will be required.

As a matter of common course, no man will offer himself, or be accepted, as a member, unless he hold our principles, and unless he be prepared to arm and fight in support of them when called upon.

But this will not be enough, else a common labourer, unable to read or write, would be eligible. Such, however, is not the principle on which we are forming this Club.

But every man is eligible and acceptable who possesses any one talent or other, or any one qualification, which would fit and enable him to be of service in any civil, military, or literary capacity, and who is willing to devote that talent or qualification to the service of his country for the next six months. It is not the *common* labour, but the *skilled* labour of the country, we desire to engage and organise in this club.

But *zeal* ranks with us as the very chief, and is, of itself alone, a sufficient qualification.

Any one who is qualified to form or lead a company, or a section of pikemen, – or who is willing to head a forlorn hope, – or who is able to address a public meeting, or who is competent to write a paragraph fit to appear in print – any and every such person will be gladly received as a member, and welcomed as a friend and comrade.

In one word, our object is to gather together a number of men competent to lead in cases of necessity, and a staff of contributors competent to take the conducting of this journal, if its present Conductors should be removed by death or exile.

We would be very desirous to name it the Felon club, but several local clubs have already adopted that name. We think they might resign it in our favour.

A Prospectus and set of rules are in preparation, which we may publish when completed.

But without waiting for such publication, we earnestly request that every man in Ireland who desires to enrol himself with us as a colleague, and comrade, and as a member of the Felon Club, will signify his wish by letter, addressed to the provisional secretary, Mr Joseph Brennan [*sic*], FELON Office, 12, Trinity-street.

Until we have obtained at least 500 members, we are resolved not to make another step in advance. If Ireland have not enough of confidence in us, or of heroism within herself, to furnish at least one member from each parish,[9] we may just as well pull down our banner at once, furl it up in a corner, or fling [it] in the dust.

JAMES F. LALOR

CHAPTER VII

'The Irish Felon', 1 July 1848
To the Confederate and Repeal Clubs in Ireland

[THE paper that follows was written in the last week of January, 1847 – just one year and five months ago – and was forwarded to one of the leading members of the Confederation, for private circulation among the council of that body. I now address it to you, just as it was written, except that I have made one or two verbal alterations, and omitted one sentence. It might possibly be better to revise and re-write it altogether, in order to adapt it more closely to the change of date, and to present conditions. But even were I to do this, there would be little to alter; and I have reasons for preferring to publish it just as it stands.

It requires to be recollected that I was addressing a particular and picked audience, and was consequently entitled to *assume* things which it would be necessary to *prove* in addressing the general public. I assume, for example, that 'moral means' alone are incompetent to achieve Repeal, because I believed that this was admitted by those I wrote for.

I see no reason to prevent me from mentioning, that in about a month from the date and delivery of my paper, I received a letter from John Mitchel, stating, that on perusal and consideration of its contents, he had fully adopted my views, and that he meant to act on them so soon as occasion should fit and serve.

It is scarcely needful to state, that the measure I wished to have substituted for a simple Repeal of the Union was – *absolute* independence, with *abolition* of the tenures by which the lands of this country are now holden in fee from the British crown.

It will be seen that the present paper was to have been followed by a second. That second was written; but it assumed the form of a private correspondence, addressed to several members of the Confederation, and to others, – the greater portion of it to John Mitchel, between whom and myself there was from the first an *almost* perfect agreement. May his fetters weigh light, and his spirit live among us!]

January 25, 1847

In putting to paper the following ideas on the course of action which the Irish Confederation ought to take, – as I am convinced it must soon and speedily fix on that course, in some more determinate shape and precise terms than it has yet thought fit to adopt, – I wish it to be understood and apparent that I do not mean, and have not time, to draw out anything that can purport to be a perfect and complete statement of my views on the subject, – and still less to exhibit in detail the principles on which they are based, or the argument in support of them. My sole wish or intention is *to suggest*. Any attempt to *convert* or *convince* would be useless. *Individuals* are never converted; they must convert themselves. Men are moved only in masses; and it is easier to convert a million of men than a single man. But neither is the attempt necessary. To you, or any other of those for whom this paper in intended, the end of the clue line is enough. You will be able, *if you choose*, to follow it out yourself. To lead you on, link by link, would be needless and absurd.

To any one who considers their speeches, resolutions, and proceedings, it will, I think, appear manifest and marked, as it does to me, that the 'seceders' have gone into organised action upon mere vague impulse and general feeling; with their objects undefined, their principles unsettled, their course unmarked; without any determinate plan, or, consequently, any fixed purpose; – for no purpose can long remain fixed, but must be ever veering and wavering, without a plan to guide, control, and sustain it; and a purpose without a plan to confine and confirm it, is no purpose at all. Such a plan, too, is wanting as a warrant and guarantee, to your-selves and to others, that your object is feasible, and your means adequate; that you have *gauged* your *enterprise* and *measured* your *means*; and that the work you call on us to do will not be wasted. There are few worse things, even in the ethics or economy of private life, than labour misdirected; but what should be said of those who would, for want of a full and exact survey and calculation, mislead and exhaust the labour, and means, and strength of a people. It is not principles alone, however pure, nor purposes the highest and noblest, that ever command success; and few will be willing to go into a ship without chart or compass, even though it steer its course by the stars of heaven.

Assuming, therefore, as I have a clear right to assume, that the leading members of the Confederation, or a certain number of them, cannot long defer coming to some agreement among them-selves as to what their objects are to be; and that some surer and better defined plan for attaining those objects must be laid down and adopted than 'sixty members, reading-rooms, and rose-water', – I proceed to submit the following considerations: –

1. Repeal, as *commonly understood*, taken by itself and STANDING ALONE, on its own mere merits and means, is an impracticable absurdity. *Impracticable*, because it cannot be effected except by means which would dissolve the connexion altogether, any means that can be used being either too feeble or too strong, – either *inadequate* or *incompatible*. *Absurd*, because both common

sense and history concur in telling us that the resulting arrangement could not possibly endure, nor be endured.

2. It is *impracticable*. It does not contain, nor can it command,
the means of possible success. It has no force to call into action on
which it can rely, whether moral, military, or mixed. Its *moral*
means, acting in the mode admitted by the constitution, and
within the limits allowed by law, are wholly incompetent; and such
as they are, they are in Mr O'Connell's possession, – to be used,
abused, or not used at all.

3. That those means are incompetent I could easily show; but
surely it is unnecessary. The fact of incompetency will, I think, at
once be recognised; or, if any one denies it, I require of him to
state, in positive and precise terms, the mode of action in which
those means can be made effective. The complete and ridiculous
failure of every such attempt ought to be evidence sufficient on
this point. The fact, briefly stated, is this, – that a 'moral agitation'
exhausts its whole power – its power of influencing opinion, and of
producing danger, damage, and inconvenience – it exhausts this
power on the country in which it takes place. It was not England,
but Ireland itself, that suffered evil and injury by our 'glorious
agitations' and 'gorgeous ethic experiments'. The most powerful
moral agitation that could be 'got up' in Ireland would not act
upon *London*. If 'emancipation' be quoted, I can prove the quotation false in application to the present case.

4. But it is no less certain that those means, whether efficient or
impotent, are, in full effect, the property of Mr O'Connell. What
may possibly have been the hasty and premature protest of the
Seceders against surrender of the Repeal question, has forced him
to adopt the policy of not giving it up *in terms*. I attach no blame to
the Seceders for this somewhat precipitate proceeding. But the
effect is, that Repeal, in its *constitutional* shape, remains still his
private property, in full, effective possession, to manage or

mismanage, to make much or little of, to sell or suspend, surrender or exchange, as best he can. The mass of the people can neither estimate nor understand the points in dispute, nor the reasons for secession; and can never be brought to join what could so easily be represented as an antagonistic and hostile movement. If any member of council doubts this opinion, I challenge him to *test it*.

5. The use of *military* means, if you had them, would be *more* than adequate. Those means would do something more than repeal the Union; nor could they be limited to any such result. This might be no objection; and I mention the fact here, not as an objection, but for another and different reason, which I need not state as yet. But, in truth, ON THIS QUESTION you possess no such means, – nor can you command or create them; – neither, even if you had them, could you employ them with success.

6. You possess no military means. Repeal is not an armed man, but a naked beggar. You fail in finding the first and fundamental element of military force, – you fail in finding *men*. The only martial population that Ireland possesses – the small farmers and farm-labourers – will never wield a weapon in favour of Repeal. This might be enough to say; – but the full and entire fact ought to be told, that you can never count again on the support of the country-peasantry in any shape or degree, on the question of Repeal. Their interest in it was never ardent; nor was it native or spontaneous, but forced and factitious. Such as it was, it is now extinct, and can never be re-created. The *small farmers*, more especially, are weary and heart-sick of Repeal, as well as of agitation, – that agitation which has been called a bloodless one, but which, *to them*, was not bloodless. You have with you on Repeal – *provided* you can take them from Mr O'Connell – the *town population* of three provinces, and a portion of that of Ulster. Such, and no more, is the *real* amount of your force. This statement may be disagreeable; and disagreeable statements are not easily believed. But you may trust in its truth,

and it requires to be made. No error could be more fatal than a false estimate of your force. But, be this true or false, in reference to *moral* means, you can never make Repeal a *military* question. You are without an army, – I need not ask, where is your arsenal?

7. But even had you those means, or if you could create them – if you had at command the whole military power of the people, and the full means of a popular armament, I say you cannot use them with effect on the question of Repeal. To make it success-ful, your fight must be a *defensive* one. The force of England is *entrenched* and *fortified*. You must draw it out of position; break up its mass; break its trained line of march and manoeuvre – its equal step and serried array. You cannot organise, or train, or discipline your own force to any point of efficiency. You must, therefore, disorganise, and untrain, and undiscipline that of the enemy; and not alone must you *unsoldier* – you must *unofficer* it also; nullify its tactique and strategy, as well as its discipline; decompose the science and system of war, and resolve them into their first elements. You must make the hostile army a mob, as your own will be; force it to act on the *offensive*, and oblige it to undertake operations for which it was never constructed. Nothing of all this could you do on *Repeal*. A Repeal-war should of necessity be an aggressive one on your part. You must be the attacking party. On all the questions involved in Repeal, England is *in occupation of the disputed points*; and you must assail them. You must send your force against armed positions, marshal your men for a stricken field, and full in its front meet England's might in unbroken mass on its ordered march. But further and finally, you must get time and licence for preparing, enlisting, organising, drilling. A REPEAL-war would have to be *prepared* in presence of the enemy. Need I point to 'Ulster on your flank'? Enough of this, and far more was needed. I doubt if a single man ever held the belief, *full and firm*, that Ireland could any time be brought to buckle a belt and march out for Repeal. The tone and

topics adopted by the *Nation* in '43 and '44 I never attributed to any thing but this – that a 'glorious agitation' *affords no poetry*, while insurrection *does*. It was the mere craving of genius for a *magnificent* subject, instead of a *mean* one.

8. There is yet another class of means and mode of force better founded in moral right, and more efficient in action, than either agitation or military insurrection. I can find no fit and defining name for it on the spur of the moment. Its theory may briefly be stated as founded on the principle of natural law, – a principle beyond dispute, denial, or doubt: –

   i.   That no man has a right to assume or claim any species of authority or jurisdiction whatsoever over any other man, against the will, or without the consent, of that other.

   ii. That should he attempt to exercise such assumed authority over another man, without his consent, that other is not bound to obey.

   iii. And that, should he take proceeding for enforcing obedience, such proceeding may be lawfully, and ought to be, resisted by any and every means and mode of force whatsoever.

This is the rigid expression of the principle in its first form; – and this principle, so expressed, is the primitive nucleus round which a nation gathers and grows. Enlarged into size and expanded into shape sufficient to give ground for a people to stand upon, and to fit it for operation, the principle I state is this, – that every distinct community or nation of men is owner of itself; and can never, of right, be bound to submit to be governed by another people.

Its practical assertion forms *the third* mode of action which this country might have recourse to; and consists: –

   i.   In refusal of obedience to usurped authority.

   ii. In maintaining and defending such refusal of obedience.

   iii. In resisting every attempt to exercise such usurped authority, and every proceeding adopted to enforce obedience.

IV. In taking quiet and peaceable possession of all the rights and powers of government, and in proceeding quietly to exercise them.

V. In maintaining and defending the exercise of such rights and powers, should it be attacked.

9. I have just thought of *a name* for this system of means, and, for want of a better, I may call it *moral insurrection*. The difference between it and *true military* insurrection amounts to nothing more, in practical effect, than the difference between the *defensive* and the *aggressive* use of physical force – a difference, however, which is often important, whether as regards moral right or mechanical efficacy.

10. As an instrument for effecting Repeal, this class of means is liable to the fatal objection stated against the preceding class. The right of moral insurrection is worthless without a military force to sustain it, and unless you be prepared and willing to use that force. On the *question of Repeal*, you have no such force. That question is *too far away* from the hearts of the peasantry. They do not *feel*, and scarcely *understand* it. They may be brought to *see its light*, but never to *feel its heat*. Other circumstances, too, render the right not available in favour of Repeal. You never could organise such an insurrection on that question. The practical assertion of the right consists of two parts: –

I. *Abolition* of British government.

II. *Formation* of a national one.

I. How would you proceed to accomplish the former? By a *general* refusal to obey the *entire* existing law? Impossible. You could not do this even *mentally* to your own satisfaction; much less could you do it in actual fact. Or by selecting and seizing some one particular law to take your stand on, trample down, and nullify? What law? Name it. The law you select for assailing must have four requisites: – first, it must form no part of the moral code; second, it must be essential to government – a part of its substance, not a mere accident – one the abrogation of which would be an abrogation of sovereignty; third, it must be one easily disobeyed; and fourth, difficult to enforce; in other words, a law that would *help* to repeal itself. There is none such to serve the purpose of *Repeal*. In Ireland, *unluckily*, there is no direct and general state-tax, payment of which might be refused and resisted.

ii. The second component part of the system – formation of a national government – is rendered impossible by the circumstance that the owners of the soil are not on your side, and are not *Irish*, but English all, in blood and feeling.

11. If those men could now at length be brought to adopt and acknowledge Ireland as their own mother-country, and to give you their adhesion and support, this latter mode of moral insurrection might be put in action with success. To try the experiment of inducing them to do so, seems to be the present policy, and *forlorn hope*, of the Confederation, and of the 'NATION'. I am quite willing to join in trying that experiment, PROVIDED it be based and conducted on the condition that the *commons* of Ireland, as well as its *nobles*, be consulted and cared for; – that the *landowners* will consent and agree to take the landholders into council – to admit them as portion of the 'Irish party' – making of that 'party' a great national league – and, finally, to frame and subscribe terms of accommodation and amnesty for the past, and articles of agreement for the future, between themselves and the tenants of the soil – one of those articles to be security of tenure in some effective shape or other to the present occupiers of land. On this basis, and on no other, would I be willing to try the experiment; but *not* to make it a 'life's labour'. Until the ___ day of _____ am I willing to try it – no longer.[10]

12. But the success of that experiment is scarce to be hoped, – especially now that the famine here has been recognised as an 'imperial calamity'; – and the policy of [the] Confederation contains, *apparently*, no *dernier resort*, – nor its proceedings any preparation for having recourse to it. The policy I wish and mean to press on your attention *does* contain such *dernier resort*; and the course of proceeding I would fain have the Confederation adopt contains, and comprises within it, the *preparatory* movement.

13. Repeal is not alone *impracticable*. As commonly understood – a simple repeal of the act of Union – it is an *absurdity*. The resulting connexion and state of things could neither endure nor be endured. Reflection tells us so, – history agrees. Two independent, co-equal, and *sovereign* Legislatures, forming one state under one crown, is an arrangement repugnant alike to common sense and experience. Reason repudiates, and history never heard of it. Two wheels in the same machine, of equal power, independent, unconnected, and not under control of the same prime mover, would form a better arrangement. Inanimate wheels, perchance, *might* work together; but under the action of human interests and passions, separate *sovereign* legislatures never could. The examples quoted in favour of such an arrangement are beneath being urged, and beneath being answered. Between Sweden and Norway it may possibly subsist, for aught I know; and it may continue to subsist, so long as the pulse of those countries continues to beat twenty per minute, and their blood remains at twenty degrees Fahrenheit. But when their atmosphere begins to beat up, and their blood to thaw and flow, – when they shall have got a *Times* in Sweden and a *Nation* in Norway; – then will the two wheels begin to clash and crash, – stop the machine, or shiver it to atoms. It subsisted between England and Ireland *for eighteen* years. But eighteen years is less in the life-time of nations than an hour in the life of man;

and as well might you urge that two quarrelsome men, ill-affected to each other, might safely and reasonably enter into partnership for life, because they had made shift to pass an hour together, without knocking each other down. And this, too, remember, was the very form of connexion which *Tone* and *Lord Edward* died to repeal, – as well as many others beside, whose *epitaph* has now, at last, been written since the 'better times' came; – that epitaph being short, sublime, and consoling, – and encouraging, too, – such as Ireland awards to her dead, – '*a gang of miscreants*'.

14. No mode of connexion between the kingdoms could be solid, desirable, or lasting, except a *federal union*, such as that existing between New York and Pennsylvania. But a federal union must be the result of *negotiation* and agreement between the federating parties. I deny the competency of the Imperial (British) Parliament to frame the act, or make the terms of federation. But, in order to negotiate, the parties must stand on equal terms, and each be *independent* of the other. *Independence*, therefore, full and entire independence, is a necessary preliminary to any permanent or satisfactory arrangement with Britain. The steps are; – independence, negotiation, federal union. What the terms should be, I will not state; – I dislike needless theorising.

15. Do not suppose I am insisting on useless *forms*. My object is very different. I think every one should familiarise his mind to the foregoing proceeding; for such *is* the proceeding, or one analogous, which must eventually be adopted. You will NEVER, in form of law, repeal the act of Union. *Never*, while the sun sits in heaven, and the laws of nature are in action. *Never*, before night goes down on the last day.

16. But a declaration of independence is yet far away, – at least in the distance that is measured by *events*, if not in the distance that is measured by *days*. I return to Repeal.

17. I sum up by again asserting that Repeal is destitute of all intrinsic force, and that, *standing alone*, on its own mere merits, it does not furnish or command the means of success.

18. Indeed, so plainly apparent is the impossibility of carrying Repeal, that its best and truest leaders are forced to throw themselves on a blind and helpless appeal to *futurity*. Broad daylight is on the present, and shows too clearly there is neither means nor hope. The future is dark; and the dark is full of shadows, which fancy may shape to what forms it will; and folly may take the phantoms to be real. But men may keep theorising and dreaming too long, – and building up, or restoring, an airy and ideal nationality, which *time* is wearing down, and wasting away, faster than they can work it up; – and when they awake from their dreams they will find, I fear, that one other people has gone out of the world, as nations and races have gone ere now.

19. For a revolution is beginning to begin which will leave Ireland *without a people*, unless it be met and conquered by a revolution which will leave it without landlords. The operation of this terrible famine will turn half the small tillage-farmers – the sole strength and hope of this island – into mere labourers working for wages. The operation of the measure of repealing the corn duties – rendered more sure and speedy by the present sudden increase of demand for foreign corn – will leave landless the remainder. Heretofore tillage land has been able to pay a higher rent than grass land. Henceforth it will be the reverse, – more especially should the potato have finally failed or disappeared. The only bar that existed to the universal removal of the small tillage-farmer – the landlord's own personal interest in retaining him – is now gone. The result is no matter of doubt; and even if it were doubtful, it ought to be provided against. Else will Ireland lose the only weapon she possesses that could conquer or cow the English government; – else, too, will she cease to have a people, – for a

population of pauperised labourers is not a people. I fear the English government, and *that English garrison* who say they own *our* soil, have a full view of their opportunity, and are determined to take advantage of it. We hear of nothing but plans and schemes to absorb surplus labour, – the surplus labour that is in process of creation. The farmers are to pass over into the condition of labourers, and to be supported during their passage. Ireland is playing out her last game, – and is she then, after all, to be check-mated, conquered, abolished? Not if her leaders and people be true, and no cravens; – true, not to any petty objects of personal distinction or personal pelf, – true, not to the foreign gang who call Ireland their own, and hold our lands by the robber's right, – but true to their country and to themselves. One move will save check-mate. By one move alone you can meet and match – and by that same you will checkmate England. One move alone can save the stakes now, – and among those stakes are the name and fame of you and yours. Men have given to you their faith, and hearts, and hopes, for your bold bearing and bold words. Even I myself am now trusting to you, and to *your* help, instead of looking round for other help and another course. Are you ready to redeem your own words, pledged in the sunshine of summer weather, – are you ready to redeem them now, in this day of sadness and storm? and to justify our faith when we followed your leading? Are you up to the mark and work of this one hour, in lieu of the 'life's labour' you promise? *Strip*, then, and bid Ireland strip. *Now or never*, – if, indeed, it be not yet too late. Oh, for one year of the bull-dog soul of England. Oh, for one year of Davis now. Whatever he may have thought *in the autumn* of '43, his voice would have now been louder than mine, to say what mine is too feeble to say. *He* would not have lain dreaming while Ireland was being trodden down, and her people conquered, finally and for ever. For England *is now actually winning her crowning and* DECISIVE victory over us and ours for ages coming.

20. To prevent this result, and at the same time to achieve independence – the only form in which Repeal can ever be carried – there is, I am convinced, but one way alone; – and that is to link Repeal to some other question, like a railway carriage to the engine; – some question possessing the intrinsic strength which Repeal wants; and strong enough to carry both itself and Repeal together, – if any such question can be found.

And such a question there is in the land. One ready prepared – ages have been preparing it. An engine ready-made – one, too, that will generate its own steam without cost or care, – a self-acting engine, if once the fire be kindled; and the fuel to kindle – the sparks for the kindling, are everywhere. Repeal had always to be *dragged*. This I speak of will *carry itself*, – as the cannon ball carries itself down the hill.

What that other question is I may possibly state, very briefly, in another paper.

Yet if its name and general character be not already known, I have lost my labour.

JAMES F. LALOR

CHAPTER VIII

'The Irish Felon', 8 July 1848
What Must Be Done

THE English Government is determined, it seems, to conquer and carry this office by quick assault or wearing siege. Of the hundred banners hoisted against England here, how comes it that the Felon-flag was the first to be assailed, and the second to be assailed? Is it deemed the most dangerous or the most defenceless, – the feeblest or the most formidable? The answer is at hand. The Castle and Conciliation Hall, the Castle and the Confederation, the Castle and one hundred Club-rooms, may stand together in this island; – the Castle and THE FELON office cannot stand together – one or other must give in or go down.

The hand of the English Government points to this journal as the foe which it hates and fears the most. If Ireland be desirous that it shall not sink, overborne by repeated assaults, there is one sure way to support and sustain it, and but one alone. I now do what I have deferred too long, – I appeal to Ireland to come to the relief of her assailed and endangered fortress; and I claim, for sake of her own success and her own safety, to have that fortress manned and provided, – its garrison increased, its defences strengthened. I demand the immediate formation of a joint-stock company to take

Mr MARTIN's place, if he should be crushed, and to continue this journal under its present or some other name.

I am proposing no new or untried idea. The *Times*, I believe, has upwards of one hundred proprietors, or had at one time; and the *Siècle* (French paper) has some thousand owners. In every undertaking and line of business, joint-stock proprietorship is taking the place and the lead of individual ownership. What is there to put the newspaper-office out of the track and operation of the same principle? The advantages of applying it in the case of 'THE FELON' are obvious, and easy to appreciate. An individual may be overborne or overawed, conquered, cowed, or corrupted, bought, banished, or beaten down; an individual may be feeble, or foolish, or fearful; an individual may be fettered, or altogether unfitted, by connections, or circumstances, or inadequate means, by private views or personal jealousies; an individual may die. A corporation or company cannot die, nor easily be conquered or committed for felony. More to show is needless. If this plan should be approved and accepted by public opinion to any efficient extent, the principles it should be carried out on are these, so far as they require to be stated now. Into details I need not enter: –

1. The company ought to be as numerous as possible, – to consist of, say, from 400 to 1,200 proprietors.

2. Every one, and each of them, should be a known and firm supporter of the felon-principles of this journal. Absolutely requisite this.

3. The shares ought each to be very low in amount: perhaps the price of each might be fixed at £1, £2, or £2 10s. Any proprietor may, perhaps, be allowed to take as many shares as he chooses, within certain limits.

4. No share to be transferable, except to a party approved and accepted by a majority of the proprietors.

5. Some one or other of the shareholders to be selected and appointed as the registered and responsible proprietor, with a salary.

6. Four or five competent editors to be engaged, or, indeed, a greater number if possible.

7. Surplus profits of the paper, beyond a certain fixed amount (reserving or replacing proprietor's capital) to be devoted to advancing the public objects for which it will have been established.

8. Englishmen and Scotchmen to be admissible as proprietors; and one, at least, of the editors to be an English Chartist, of known talent and honesty. He must, of course, be strictly felonious, and fully prepared to aid, and abet, and assist in a 'premature insurrection', within the next one hundred years at farthest, as we cannot possibly afford to admit any of those doubtful characters into the establishment who first help to blow up a flame, and then help to blow it out by the free and easy use of the words '*premature*', 'incendiary', &c.

Into further explanation or detail it is needless to go for the present.

Am I fully understood? It is needless to say more. Am I half understood? – it is sufficient. I can make or enable no man to *think* – I can only help him.

There may possibly be objections or impediments to this scheme, which I have overlooked. If so, I desire to be made acquainted with them; and also to be aided by suggestions for making it more efficient. These I respectfully request to have stated, as briefly as possible, by letter (and not otherwise), addressed to Mr Joseph Brenan, FELON-Office, Trinity-street. The letters must be short. A longer letter than two pages of note-paper, I never read, more especially if it be eloquently written. I hate eloquence on all subjects, particularly on *little* subjects.

Immediate written applications and proposals, absolute or conditional (addressed to Mr Brenan), are requested from parties desirous to become shareholders in the undertaking.

Form the company I propose, and then – before they 'squelch' Ireland, they must 'squelch' the FELON-Office. Ha! 'squelch it – by heavens – squelch' it!'[†] It is good. No middle course can answer that. Your knee to the ground – or death and defiance, oh Ireland!

JAMES F. LALOR

[†] 'Ireland is like a half-starved rat, that crosses the path of an elephant. What must the elephant do? Squelch it – by heavens – squelch it.' *Late Letter of Thomas Carlyle.*

CHAPTER IX

'The Irish Felon', 8 July 1848

The Faith of a Felon

BY JAMES F. LALOR

WHEN MR DUFFY expected arrest, some weeks ago, he drew up his profession of principles, 'The Creed of *The Nation*'. Under influence of similar feelings and considerations, though not exactly the same, nor excited by circumstances altogether alike, I hasten to put my own principles upon record. Until yesterday I did not intend to have done this for some weeks to come. The statement or confession of faith that follows I could have wished for time to make more correct and complete. It is ill-framed, ill-connected, and wants completeness. But, even such as it stands, I do firmly believe that it carries the fortunes of Ireland; – and even such as it stands, I now send it forth to its fate, to conquer or be conquered. It may be master of Ireland and make her a Queen; it may lie in the dust and perish with her people.

Here, then, is the confession and faith of a FELON.

Years ago I perceived that the English conquest consisted of two parts combined into one whole, – the conquest of our liberties, the conquest of our lands.

I saw clearly that the re-conquest of our liberties would be incomplete and worthless without the re-conquest of our lands, – would not, necessarily, involve or produce that of our lands, and could not, on its own means, be possibly achieved; while the re-conquest of our lands would involve the other – would, at least, be complete in itself, and adequate to its own purposes; and could *possibly*, if not easily, be achieved.

The lands were *owned* by the conquering race, or by traitors of the conquered race. They were *occupied* by the native people, or by settlers who had mingled and merged.

I selected, as the *mode* of re-conquest, – to refuse payment of rent, and resist process of ejectment.

In that mode I determined to effect the re-conquest, and staked on it all my hopes, here and hereafter, – my hopes of an effective life and an eternal epitaph.

I was biding my time when the potato-failure hurried a crisis. The landlords and English government took instant advantage of the famine, and the small occupiers began to quit in thousands. I saw that Ireland was to be won at once, or lost for ever. I felt her slipping from under my feet, with all her hopes and all my own, – her lights quenching, her arm withering.

It almost seemed to me as if the Young Ireland party, the quarrel, the secession, the Confederation, had all been specially pre-ordained and produced in order to aid me. My faith in the men who formed the Council of that body was then unbounded. My faith in them still is as firm as ever, though somewhat more measured. In the paper I published last week, and in a private correspondence that ensued with some of its members, I proposed they should merge the Repeal question in a mightier project – that of wresting this island from English rule altogether, in the only mode in which it could possibly be achieved. I endeavoured to show them they were only keeping up a feeble and ineffectual fire from a foolish distance, upon the *English Government*, which stands out of reach and beyond our power; and urged them to wheel their batteries round and bend them on the *English garrison* of landlords, who stand here within our hands, scattered, isolated, and helpless, girdled round by the might of a people. Except two or three of them, all refused at the time, and have persisted in refusing until now. They wanted an alliance with the landowners. They chose to consider them as Irishmen, and imagined they could induce them to hoist the green flag. They wished to preserve an Aristocracy. They desired, not a *democratic*, but a merely *national* revolution. Who imputes blame to them for this? Whoever does so will not have me to join him. I have no feeling but one of respect for the motives that caused reluctance and delay. That delay, however, I consider as matter of deep regret. Had the Confederation, in the May or June of '47, thrown heart, and mind, and means, and might, into the movement I pointed out, they would have made it successful, and settled for once and for ever all quarrels and questions between us and England. I repeat my expression of strong regret that they should not have adopted this course, instead of persisting in a protracted and abortive effort, at a most dangerous conjuncture, to form an alliance of *bargain* and *barter* with our hereditary and inveterate enemies, between whom and the people of this island there will never be a peace, except the peace of death or of desolation. Regrets, however, are useless now.

The opinions I then stated, and which I yet stand firm to, are these: –

1. That, in order to save their own lives, the occupying tenants of the soil of Ireland ought, next autumn, to refuse all rent and arrears of rent then due, beyond and except the value of the overplus of harvest produce remaining in their hands after having deducted and reserved a due and full provision for their own subsistence during the next ensuing twelve months.

2. That they ought to refuse and resist being made beggars, landless and houseless, under the English law of ejectment.

3. That they ought further, *on principle*, to refuse ALL rent to the

present usurping proprietors, until the people, the true proprietors (or lords paramount, in legal parlance), have, in national congress or convention, decided *what* rents they are to pay, and *to whom* they are to pay them.

4. And that the people, on grounds of *policy* and *economy*, ought to decide (as a general rule, admitting of reservations) that those rents shall be paid *to themselves*, the people, for public purposes, and for behoof and benefit of them, the entire general people.

These are the principles, as clearly and fully stated as limit of time will allow, which I advise Ireland to adopt at once, and at once to arm for. Should the people accept and adhere to them, the English government will then have to choose whether to surrender the Irish landlords, or to support them with the armed power of the empire.

If it refuse to incur the odium and expense, and to peril the safety of England in a social war of extermination, then the landlords are nobody, the people are lords of the land, a mighty social revolution is accomplished, and the foundations of a national revolution surely laid. If it should, on the other hand, determine to come to the rescue and relief of its garrison, – elect to force their rents and enforce their rights by infantry, cavalry, and cannon, and attempt to lift and carry the whole harvest of Ireland – a somewhat *heavy* undertaking, which might become a *hot* one, too, – then I, at least, for one, am prepared to bow with humble resignation to the dispensations of Providence. Welcome be the will of God. We must only try to keep our harvest, to offer a peaceful, passive resistance, to barricade the island, to break up the roads, to break down the bridges, – and, should need be, and favourable occasions offer, surely we may venture to try the steel. Other approved modes of moral resistance might gradually be added to these, according as we should become trained to the system: and all combined, I imagine, and well worked, might possibly task the strength and break the heart of the empire.

Into *artistic* details, however, I need not, and do not choose, to enter for the present.

It has been said to me that such a war, on the principles I propose, would be looked on with detestation by Europe. I assert the contrary: I say such a war would propagate itself throughout Europe. Mark the words of this prophecy: – The principle I propound goes to the foundations of Europe, and, sooner or later, will cause Europe to outrise. Mankind will yet be masters of the earth. The right of the people to make the laws – this produced the first great modern earthquake, whose latest shocks, even now, are heaving in the heart of the world. The right of the people to own the land, – this will produce the next. Train your hands, and your sons' hands, gentlemen of earth, for you and they will yet have to use them. I want to put Ireland foremost, in the van of the world, at the head of the nations, – to set her aloft in the blaze of the sun, and to make her for ages the load star [*sic*] of history. Will she take the path I point out, – the path to be free, and famed, and feared, and followed, – the path that goes sunward? Or, onward to the end of time, will wretched Ireland ever come limping and lagging hindmost? Events must answer that. It is a question I almost fear to look full in the face. The soul of this island seems to sink where that of another country would soar. The people sank and surrendered to the famine instead of growing savage, as any other people would have done.

I am reminded that there are few persons now who trouble themselves about the 'conquest'; and there may be many – I know there are some – who assent to the two first of the four principles I have stated, and are willing to accept them as the grounds of an armed movement; but who object to the two last of them. I am advised to summon the land-tenants of Ireland to stand up in battle-array for an armed struggle in defence of their rights of life and subsistence, without asserting any greater or more comprehensive right. I distinctly refuse to do so. I refuse to narrow the case and claim of this island into any such petty dimensions, or to found it on the rogue's or the beggar's plea, the plea of necessity. Not as a starving bandit, or desperate beggar, who demands, to save life, what does not belong to him, do I wish Ireland to stand up, but as a decrowned Queen, who claims back her own with an armed hand. I attest and urge the plea of utter and desperate necessity to fortify her claim, but not to found it. I rest it on no temporary and passing conditions, but on principles that are permanent, and imperishable, and universal; – available to all times and all countries, as well as to our own, – I pierce through the upper stratum of occasional and shifting circumstance to bottom and base on the rock below. I put the question in its eternal form, – the form in which, how often soever suppressed for a season, it can never be finally subdued, but will remain and return, outliving and outlasting the corruption and cowardice of generations. I view it as ages will view it – not through the mists of a famine, but by the living lights of the firmament. You may possibly be induced to reject it in the form I propose, and accept it in the other. If so, you will accept the question, and employ it as a weapon against England, in a shape and under conditions which deprive it of half its strength. You will take and work it fettered and hand-cuffed – not otherwise. To take it in its *might*, you must take it in its *magnitude*. I propose you should take Sampson into your service. You assent: but insist that his locks shall be shorn. You, moreover, diminish and degrade it down from a *national* into a mere *class* question. In the form *offered*, it would carry independence – in the form accepted, it will not even carry Repeal, in its minimum of meaning. You fling away Repeal, when you fling away the *only* mode of achieving it. For by force of arms alone can it ever be

The Faith of a Felon

achieved; – and never, on the Repeal question, will you see men stand in array of battle against England.

I trouble myself as little as any one does about the 'conquest' as taken abstractedly – as an affair that took place long ages ago. But that 'conquest' is still in existence, with all its rights, claims, laws, relations, and results. The landlord holds his lands by right and title of conquest, and uses his powers as only a conqueror may. The tenant holds under the law of conquest, – *vae victis*.

Public policy must be founded on public principle; and the question of *ethics* must be settled before the question of *economy* can be taken up or touched. If the Irish landlord's title be valid and good, no considerations of policy or economy could make a refusal to pay rent appear anything better than robbery.

What founds and forms the right of property in land? I have never read in the direction of that question. I have all my life been destitute of books. But from the first chapter of Blackstone's second book, the only page I ever read on the subject, I know that jurists are unanimously agreed in considering 'first occupancy' to be the only true original foundation of the right of property and possession of land.

Now, I am prepared to prove that 'occupancy' wants every character and quality that could give it moral efficacy as a foundation of right. I am prepared to prove this, when 'occupancy' has first been *defined*. If no definition can be given, I am relieved from the necessity of showing any claim founded on occupancy to be weak and worthless.

Refusing, therefore, at once, to accept or recognise this feeble and fictitious title of occupancy, which was merely *invented by theorists*, and which, in actual fact, was never respected and never pleaded, I proceed at once to put my own principles in order and array.

To any plain understanding the right of private property is very simple. It is the right of man to possess, enjoy, and transfer, the substance and use of whatever *he has himself* CREATED. This title is good against the world; and it is the *sole* and *only* title by which a valid right of absolute private property can possibly vest.

But no man can plead any such title to a right of property in the substance of the soil.

The earth, together with all it *spontaneously* produces, is the free and common property of all mankind, of natural right, and by the grant of God; – and, all men being equal, no man, therefore, has a right to appropriate exclusively to himself any part or portion thereof, except with and by the *common consent* and *agreement* of all other men.

The sole original right of property in land which I acknowledge to be *morally* valid, is this right of common consent and agreement. Every other I hold to be fabricated and fictitious, null, void, and of no effect.

In the original and natural state of mankind, existing in independent families, each man must, in respect of actual fact, either *take* and *hold* (ASSUME OCCUPANCY as well as *maintain possession of*) his land by right and virtue of such consent and agreement as aforesaid, with all those who might be in a position to dispute and oppose his doing so; or he must take and maintain possession *by force*. The fictitious right of occupancy – invented by jurists to cover and account for a state of settlement otherwise unaccountable and indefensible on moral principles – this right would be utterly worthless, and could seldom accrue; for except in such a case as that of a single individual thrown on a desert island, the *question of right* would generally arise, and require to be settled, *before* any colourable 'title by occupancy' could be established, or even actual occupation be effected. And then – *what constitutes* occupancy? What length of possession gives 'title by occupancy'?

When independent families have united into separate tribes, and tribes swelled into nations, the same law obtains; – each tribe or nation has but either one or other of two available rights to stand upon, – they must take and maintain territorial possession by consent and agreement with all other tribes and nations; or they must take and hold by the *tenure of chivalry*, in the right of their might.

In either of these two modes – that of conquest or that of common agreement – have the distribution and settlement of the lands of every country been made. Occupancy, indeed, and forsooth! Messrs BLACKSTONE, TITIUS, LOCKE and Co. Occupancy against the Goth, – occupancy before the trampling hoofs of ATTILA, – occupancy to stop HOUSTON or TAYLOR.

In every country the condition and character of the people tell whether it was by conquest or common agreement that the existing settlement and law of landed property were established.

When it is made by agreement there will be equality of distribution; which equality of distribution will remain permanent, within certain limits. For, under natural laws, landed property has rather a tendency to divide than to accumulate.

When the independent families who form the natural population of a country compose and organise into a regular community, the imperfect compact, or agreement, by which each man holds his land must necessarily assume the more perfect shape of a *positive and precise grant from the people*, just as *all his other rights* must be defined and ascertained, – and just as all other vague rules of agreement must organise into *laws*. That grant must, necessarily, assume and establish the general and common right of all the people, as joint and co-equal proprietors of all the land; – for such grant will be, of itself, an act of exercising and proceeding upon that right.

That grant, and all other grants, must also, of necessity, without any express words, reserve the general right of the people as first proprietors and *lords paramount*, and give nothing more than a right of use and occupancy; – and it must, furthermore, recognise

and reserve, in like manner, the permanent right of the people for
ever to revise, alter, and amend the mode and condition of settlement then made, – and to modify or withdraw all grants made
upon, or in pursuance of, that mode and condition of settlement.
[For no generation of living men can bind a generation that is yet
unborn, or can sell or squander the rights of man; and each
generation of men has but a life-interest in the world. But no
generation continues the same for one hour together. Its identity is
in perpetual flux. From whence it follows that, practically: –][11]

Any condition of settlement established, and all grants made
thereupon, may, *at any time* thenceforth, be questioned, re-con-
sidered, revised, altered, or amended.

And in order, therefore, to render the settlement a permanent
one, it would be requisite to make it such as would give the majority
and mass of the people a permanent interest in its maintenance.

But that object could not be accomplished by granting away the
whole of the land to one man, or to *eight thousand* men, in absolute,
irresponsible ownership for ever, without condition of paying
rent, or any other condition whatsoever. This would be a settlement beyond the authority and right of any generation to make.
Those deriving under it could be only considered as holding
forcible possession, which any succeeding generation would have
the clear right of ousting. And the people would either rise against
such settlement, and trample it down, – or sink under it into slaves.

Putting together and proceeding on the principles now stated,
it will appear that, if those principles be sound, no man can
legitimately claim possession or occupation of any portion of land
or any right of property therein, except by grant from the people,
at the will of the people, as tenant to the people, and on terms and
conditions made or sanctioned by the people; – and that every
right, except the right so created and vesting by grant from the

people, is nothing more or better than the right of the robber who holds forcible possession of what does not lawfully belong to him.

The present proprietors of Ireland do not hold or claim by grant from the people, nor even – except in Ulster – by any species of imperfect agreement or assent of the people. They got and keep their lands in the robber's right – the right of conquest – in despite, defiance, and contempt of the people. Eight thousand men are owners of this entire island, – claiming the right of enslaving, starving, and exterminating eight millions. We talk of asserting free-government, and of ridding ourselves of foreign domination – while, lo! eight thousand men are lords of our lives, – of us and ours, blood and breath, happiness or misery, body and soul. Such is the state of things in every country where the settlement of the lands has been effected by *conquest*. In Ulster the case is somewhat different, *much* to the advantage of the people, but not so much as it ought to have been. Ulster was not merely *conquered*, but *colonised*, – the native race being expelled, as in the United States of America: – and the settlement that prevails was made by a sort of consent and agreement among the conquering race.

No length of time or possession can sanction claims acquired by robbery, or convert them into valid rights. The people are still rightful owners, though not in possession. '*Nullum tempus occurrit Deo, – nullum tempus occurrit populo.*'[12]

In many countries besides this, the lands were acquired, and long held, by right of force or conquest. But in most of them the settlement and laws of conquest have been abrogated, amended, or modified, to a greater or lesser extent. In some, an outrise of the people has trampled them down, – in some, the natural laws have triumphed over them, – in some, a despotic monarch or minister has abolished or altered them. In Ireland alone they remain unchanged, unmitigated, unmollified, in all their original ferocity and cruelty, and the people of Ireland must now abolish them, or be themselves abolished, and this is *now* the *more urgent* business.

[We are compelled, from want of space, to postpone the remaining portion of Mr Lalor's paper to our next publication.]

CHAPTER X

'The Irish Felon', 15 July 1848
Resistance

SINCE the present contest began, it is eighteen years; and eighteen years makes a long period, and large portion, in the lifetime of one generation. Since it began, youth has grown grey, and manhood gone far to the grave. It must now, at length, from sheer necessity, be brought to a quick determination, whether for or against us; nor it must cease altogether, and for ever. It can neither sustain itself, nor be sustained any longer. And, for myself I will say this, that I choose utter and eternal defeat rather than to have it last for even one year more. As hitherto conducted, it has been the most disastrous and disgraceful in character and results that a nation of men was ever engaged in. It has been withering all our hearts, and wasting out our very souls: – sapping all our virtues, strengthening all our vices, and making new vices of its own. It has gone far, and well nigh succeeded, in cowardising a brave race, and turning a nation of heroes into a nation of cravens. An age of the worst tyranny of England's worst times would be better than another year of it. Human nature itself can bear such a burthen no longer, and is sickening and sinking under it fast, longing to relieve, and, if possible, to redeem itself. I pronounce and record my own vote to have it end. If we be able to win, let us go in and win at once. If it be otherwise, let us submit and surrender, and ask for the mercies and peace that tyranny grants to slaves.

There was force enough in this island to have brought this contest to a successful issue at any time. Not deficiency of force, but disunion, dishonesty, defect of courage, and faults of conduct, have prevented this; for the result of thorough and determined resistance could not possibly be doubtful for a single week.

Among the many causes that have been hitherto in combination to produce failure and defeat, the one which now demands especial notice is this, – that every position occupied by the people has been surrendered as soon as assailed, and every movement abandoned when met by resistance. This, in fact, has come now to be a fixed habit of action, counted and calculated on by our enemies; if, indeed, it be not natural to us, rather than formed – a matter of melancholy doubt. Irishmen, apparently, are cowed and conquered just at the very point where an Englishman only begins to be thoroughly roused, and to fight savagely; and more wanted, I fear, and better worth for us than a pike in every hand, would be three drops of English blood in every heart – the bull-dog blood that will not sink, but boils the higher for every blow.

In the history of every successful struggle by a nation or a people against foreign rule or domestic tyranny, one impulse and principle of action is read in every page. Wherever the force of the government was bent, there, too, the people banded their force to meet it. The point of assault became the post to rally. No position was abandoned, no inch of ground was given. The attack was the signal and summons, not of surrender, but of instant, obstinate, and stern resistance. This is the road to victory, – the high road; the only road that can never lead astray; the road from which every diverging bye-way leads to defeat; the road that reason points out, and nature itself, and all the principles that reason acts on, and all the passions that nature owns. This is the road, and a people who can be persuaded to persist in following any other were made to be beaten, trodden down, and trampled on. Let men differ as they may about other principles, there is one that admits of no dispute, and can never be relinquished without relinquishing manhood and all its rights: the great first principle of – BLOW FOR BLOW; blow for blow in self-defence, – no matter for why or wherefore, no matter for risk or result.

And now: –

The official authorities of the English government have assailed this journal and two others – the *Nation* and *Tribune* – with the clear intent, as declared by their acts, of crushing those journals, and smothering down the voice of the Irish people, by naked force, violence, and terror, not even disguised under forms of law, and in open violation of all those public and private rights of liberty, property, and security, which they profess to defend, guard, and guarantee.

Those rights we are firmly resolved on defending, and we appeal to the people of Ireland to aid us in their defence.

The Empire has declared to crush us, and we have determined to league in self-defence, and stand up to the Empire. I speak for the *Nation*, I speak for the *Tribune*, I speak for THE FELON. We stand up in firm defence and full defiance.

We have determined to cease publication of the three journals named, and to establish another, or rather three others, the prospectus of which will be published in a few days.

But the means and resources at our command, or at the command of any small number of private individuals, would be altogether unequal to the contest we shall have to sustain; and we, therefore, request the instant formation of a company, with a paid-up capital of, at least, £2,000, to be subscribed in shares of £1 each, for the purpose of establishing the proposed journal, and of making the requisite arrangements for its general conduct and management.

Unless this be done, and until it be done, I, for one of many, shall continue mute on every other matter. One thing at a time, – one thing alone, until it be finished; and here is what is first in order, importance, and necessity. If Ireland will for ever, or for even one day longer, go on talking, determining, and declaring, without doing any one thing practical that is proposed to her, I quit her service; and so, too, will many others beside. We don't choose to get ourselves transported, or, what is worse, get ourselves laughed at, for mere idle words, that spend themselves on empty space.

The general principles on which the proposed undertaking is to be founded are stated in a paper which I published in last week's FELON, and out of which I now re-publish them. The specific rules and arrangements I have neither any reason, nor, of course, any right, to undertake stating. They must be determined by consideration and agreement of the joint proprietors themselves, at their first, or some subsequent meeting.

1. The company ought to be as numerous as possible, – to consist of, say, from 400 to 1,200 proprietors.
2. Every one, and each of them, should be a known and firm supporter of the felon-principles of this journal. Absolutely requisite this.
3. The shares ought each to be very low in amount: perhaps the price of each might be fixed at £1, £2, or £2 10s. Any proprietor may, perhaps, be allowed to take as many shares as he chooses, within certain limits.
4. No share to be transferable, except to a party approved and accepted by a majority of the proprietors.
5. Some one or other of the shareholders to be selected and appointed as the registered and responsible proprietor, with a salary.

6. Four or five competent editors to be engaged, or, indeed, a greater number if possible.

7. Surplus profits of the paper, beyond a certain fixed amount (reserving or replacing proprietor's capital) to be devoted to advancing the public objects for which it will have been established.

8. Englishmen and Scotchmen to be admissible as proprietors; and one, at least, of the editors to be an English Chartist, of known talent and honesty. He must, of course, be strictly felonious, and fully prepared to aid, abet, and assist in a 'premature insurrection', within the next hundred years at farthest.

A committee is in course of formation, for the purpose of receiving applications and proposals from parties desirous of becoming shareholders. When formed, the names will be published, together with the prospectus.

JAMES F. LALOR

CHAPTER XI

'The Irish Felon', 22 July 1848
Clearing Decks

IT is never the mass of a people that forms its real and efficient might. It is the men by whom that mass is moved and managed. All the great acts of history have been done by a very few men. Take half a dozen names out of any revolution upon record, and what would have been the result?

Not Scotland, but Wallace, barred and baffled Edward. Not England, but Cromwell, struck a king from his seat. Not America, but six or eight American men, put stripes and stars on the banner of a nation. To quote examples, however, is needless. They must strike at once on every mind.

If Ireland be conquered now, – or what would be worse, if she fails to fight, – it will certainly not be the fault of the people at large, – of those who form the rank and file of the nation. The failure and fault will be that of those who have assumed to take the office of commanding and conducting the march of a people for liberty, without, perhaps, having any commission from nature to do so, or natural right, or acquired requisite. The general population of this island are ready to find and furnish everything which can be demanded from the mass of a people, – the numbers, the physical strength, the animal daring, the health, hardihood, and endurance. No population on earth of equal amount would furnish a more effective military conscription. We want only competent leaders – men of courage and capacity – men whom nature meant and made for leaders – not the praters, and pretenders, and bustling botherbys of the old agitation. Those leaders are yet to be found. Can Ireland furnish them? It would be a sheer and absurd blasphemy against nature to doubt it. The first blow will bring them out.

But very many of our present prominent leaders must first retire or be dismissed. These men must at once be got rid of utterly. They *must*. There is nothing else for it. They are stopping our way, clinging round our arms, giving us up to our enemies. Many of them came into this business from the mere desire of gaining little personal distinctions on safe terms and at a cheap and easy rate, – of obtaining petty honours and offices, – of making a small Dublin reputation, – of creating a parish fame, or a tea-table fame. They will never suffer the national movement to swell beyond the petty dimensions which they are able, themselves, to manage and command; and are, therefore, a source not of strength, but of weakness, – and the source of all our weakness. But for them we could walk down the utmost force of England in one month.

In a movement of the nature [of that] which has been going on for years in this country, it was impossible to prevent the intrusion into offices of command of that class of men who mar success instead of making it. Indeed it was into their hands those offices have been almost exclusively confided up to the present hour. This can hardly be called a mistake, for it was unavoidable. The movement, naturally and of necessity, belonged to them. It was of the mock-heroic order, the machinery of which none but mean hands would undertake or be competent to manage. The class of men who make Revolutions, and who doubtless exist here as well as elsewhere, have been altogether disgusted and driven away from the service of their country by the peculiar character of that sort of 'struggle for freedom', the system of 'moral agitation' which Ireland thought fit to adopt; and from which their pride of manhood and pride of country revolted. The staff of leaders which that system created, and has left behind it, is composed of men utterly unfit and unwilling to take charge of a military struggle, and who ought at once to be superseded and replaced. For two generations – may history forget to mention them! – those men have been working to do this, – the best work that ever yet was done for tyranny, – to take from the people the terror of their name, and make popular movement a mockery. And what now are they working to do? To hold Ireland down, hand and foot, while her chains are being locked and double-locked; and her four noble prisoners sent fettered and hand-cuffed to a penal colony of England – hear it O Earth and hear it O GOD! – for saying that Ireland should suffer famine no more. Oh! worse for us than the foreign tyrant is the native traitor; and worse than the open traitor in the enemy's ranks is the vile trickster and the base craven in our own. Away with them! They must quit at once or be quashed. One man, and every man, of those now in the prison of Newgate, is worth a host of the dastards and drivellers who are bidding you stand by and 'bide your time', while your best and bravest are being transported as felons in the face of your city, in the sight of two islands, and in view of all earth.

But how are you to know them, those menials of England in the green livery of their country? By this shall ye know them. Any man who objects to every plan of armed resistance that is proposed, while he produces none, or no better one, of his own. Or any man who tells you that an act of armed resistance – even if made so soon as to-morrow – even if offered by ten men only – even if offered by men armed only with stones – any man who tells you that even such an act of resistance would be premature, imprudent, or dangerous, – any and every such man should at once be spurned and spit at. For, remark you this, and recollect it – that *somewhere*, and *somehow*, and by *somebody*, a *beginning must be* made; and that the *first* act of resistance is always, and must be ever, premature, imprudent, and dangerous. Lexington was premature, Bunker's Hill was imprudent, and even Trenton was dangerous.[13]

There are men who speak much to you of prudence and caution, and very little of any virtue beside. But every vice may call itself by the name of some one virtue or other; and of prudence there are many sorts. Cowardice may call itself, and readily pass for, caution; and of those who preach prudence, it behoves to inquire what kind of prudence it is they speak of, and to what class of prudent persons they belong themselves. There is a prudence the virtue of the wisest and bravest, – there is a prudence the virtue of beggars and slaves. Which class do those belong to who are prating now for prudence, and against premature insurrection; while rejecting every proceeding and plan for preparation?

Against the advice of those men, and all men such as they, I declare my own. In the case of Ireland now, there is but *one fact* to deal with, and *one question* to be considered. *The fact* is this, – that there are at present in occupation of our country some 40,000 armed men, in the livery and service of England; and *the question* is, – how best and soonest to kill and capture those 40,000 men.

If required to state my own individual opinion, and allowed to choose my own time, I certainly would take the time when the full harvest of Ireland shall be stacked in the haggards. But not unfrequently GOD selects and sends his own seasons and occasions; and oftentimes, too, an enemy is able to force the necessity of either fighting or failing. In the one case, we ought not, in the other we surely cannot, attempt waiting for our harvest-home. If opportunity offers, we must dash at that opportunity – if driven to the wall, we must wheel for resistance. Wherefore, let us fight in September, if we may – but sooner, if we must.

Meanwhile, however, remember this, – that somewhere, and somehow, and by somebody, a beginning must be made. Who strikes the first blow for Ireland? Who draws first blood for Ireland? Who wins a wreath that will be green for ever?

J. F. L.

Notes to Lalor's Articles

1   Ralph Bernal Osborne (1808–82), advanced Liberal MP.

2   The Labour Rate Act (1846) intended to provide employment to the poor and increase the amount of land under cultivation by granting government advances to landlords towards improving their estates. These advances, however, would have to be repaid through special local taxes.

3   'Landlords' in the original.

4   The Reproductive Employment Committee was set up by a number of landlords in late 1846 in order to resist government relief legislation and campaign for amendments. One of their main demands was that government funding should be applied to useful, 'reproductive' works that would help to produce food (see resolutions, *Nenagh Guardian*, 16 Jan. 1847). In June 1847 they renamed themselves as the Irish Council.

5   33 Geo. III, *c.29, An Act to prevent the Election or Appointment of unlawful assemblies, under pretence of preparing or presenting public Petitions or other Addresses to His Majesty, or the Parliament.*

6   Conciliation Hall was the Dublin headquarters of the Repeal Association.

7   The idea for a Council of Three Hundred was first mooted by O'Connell during his monster-meeting campaign of 1842, and was again taken up by Young Ireland in the context of the 1848 revolutions. The plan was to defy the Convention Act and repeat the Volunteers' 1782 feat by bringing together a nationwide assembly of representatives in order to put pressure on the British government. More particularly in this case, the council was intended to serve as the basis for the future Irish parliament.

8   O'Connell's monster meeting at the Hill of Tara, which took place on 15 Aug. 1843.

9   The number of Irish Catholic parishes was set at 1,080 in 1871 (Jeremiah Newman, 'The Priests of Ireland: A Socio-Religious Survey. I. Numbers and Distribution', *The Irish Ecclesiastical Record* XCVIII: 5 (1962), pp. 1–27; p. 6.

10   Probably 1 September 1847. Thomas P. O'Neill, *James Fintan Lalor*, trans. John T. Goulding (Dublin, 2003), p. 63.

11   Brackets in the original.

12   'God is not subject to time; the people are not subject to time.'

13   Three of the battles in the War of American Independence.

Appendices

Unpublished documents

<u>Private</u>

Miss Butler's
Maryborough

Sir. –

I address you on a subject of the greatest interest and importance, – of as much interest and importance to *me*, or to the humblest individual in Ireland, as it can possibly be even to *you*; – and from no motive but that of doing what I consider may be a great, though a silent and humble, service to the country I belong to; yet it is with much hesitation that I venture to do so, because I am not at all sure that either my subject or motives will be considered a sufficient apology for intruding on your time. –

I have long seen and felt – (what every man who retains, in this most *contagious* country, the use of his own mind, and of his own senses, to see, to hear, and to judge for himself, perceives) – the absolute necessity which exists, that *all* agitation for political objects

† British Library Peel Papers Addenda, MS 40530, ff 399–400v.

should entirely cease, before any improvement can be effected in the condition of the Irish people. I am most anxious that the present Repeal-movement should be speedily and safely suppressed, – not imperfectly and for a period, but fully and for ever.

To effect that object I wish to contribute whatever little aid it may be in my power to give. I am firmly convinced that on the course of proceeding which her Majesty's Government may adopt in dealing with this agitation, depends the state of this country for very many years. I know that their course will be determined and formed upon the evidence before them.

I am ignorant of the sources from whence that evidence may be derived, and of the extent and character of the information which is in their possession, or at their command. I am inclined to fear, however, that it may possibly not be such as can altogether be relied upon for ennabling [*sic*] her Majesty's Government to see the facts of the present movement in their true dimensions and colours, or to form a correct estimate of the effects likely to follow any particular line of action. I cannot help considering that *I* am, – from facilities of *position*, and other circumstances, – better acquainted with the existing movement, – its extent, strength, leaders, motives, means, and intentions, – than most, or, perhaps, than any one, of those whose means of information are at the service of her Majesty's Ministers. I can scarcely conceive, more especially, that any person holding an official situation can possibly know the agitation or the agitators so thoroughly and truly as I do. They see only the *exterior* of that agitation, – I see its *interior*. I live *within* it. My father, and family, and most of my near relatives, are actively engaged in it. I wish to furnish you with whatever information I am possessed of, – so far as I think it may be of any importance in directing your course; but I am not aware by what rule her Majesty's Government are guided in receiving, – or to what extent, or in what manner, they may be willing to receive, – or whether they may consent at all to receive, – information from any others than the local authorities. I am not at all desirous of doing what might – if done without being authorised, – be very justly considered as an intrusion and an impertinence.

May I therefore request your permission to communicate to you such facts respecting the present agitation and the probable results of the several modes of proceeding which her Majesty's Government may adopt in reference to it, as I think it may be of any consequence that you should be put in possession of. –

If there be any particular points on which her Majesty's Government may be desirous of information, and if specific questions be put to me on these points, I will answer them as fully as I can; – provided, of course, that such questions be of a general nature, not in reference to individuals. –

I address *you* rather than Sir James Graham, because I do not consider that such a matter as the existing movement in this country belongs more peculiarly to any one minister of the Crown than to another; – or, if it do, that it is to that minister who is the reputed head of the Administration. If, however, a strict adherence to *forms* be necessary, or be preferred, – be good enough to let me be informed whether I may address my statement to Sir James Graham, – in order to prevent the necessity of having to write for his formal permission, and the consequent loss of time, which a simple reference to the Home-Secretary would involve.

I mark this letter as 'private', simply because my family-friends are all violent Repealers. But it is only in *Ireland* that I wish it to be considered as 'private'; – and that merely for the present, as it is probable that I shall soon be *obliged* to join the Conservative party openly and actively.

Let your answer be addressed to, – James F. Lalor. – care of Miss Butler – Maryborough.

I have the honour to remain Sir

Your obedient Servant,

James F. Lalor

P. S. Though my name is subscribed to this letter, – yet, without some explanation, it would, to *you*, be an *anonymous* one. I beg to state, therefore, that I am a son of Mr P. Lalor, of Tenakill, in the Queen's County, who was one of the representatives for that County in Parliament, some years since; – and who then was, and, I regret to say, still continues, a zealous and active Repealer. It was he who first planned and proposed the late system of passive resistance to the collection of Tithes. He belongs to the highest class of what, in this country, are called 'Gentlemen-farmers'; – so that, as regards station in society, I am placed pretty nearly at the *point of contact*, where all ranks of Repealers *touch*. I was, myself, at one time, something *more* than a mere Repealer, in private feeling; – but Mr O'Connell, *his agitators*, and his series of wretched agitations, first *disgusted* me into a conservative in point of *feeling*; and reflection and experience have *converted* me into one in point of *principle*. I have been *driven* into the conviction, more strongly confirmed by every day's experience, that it is only to a Conservative Government, to her landed proprietors, and to *peace*, that this country can look for any improvement in her social condition.

I have now furnished you with all the particulars of information which I think necessary to ennable [*sic*] you to judge how far reliance may be placed on the statements I wish to make, – so far as my opportunities of obtaining correct information, and of forming a correct judgement, are concerned. As to my wish and intention to make only *true* statements, and my honesty of purpose in making them, you must, in forming your opinion, depend in a great measure, for the present, on whatever internal evidence the statements themselves may afford, if you be willing to receive them. – I address to Privy Gardens, – not knowing whether I act correctly in so doing.

JFL

Right Hon. Sir Robert Peel

A NEW NATION[‡]
AGRICULTURAL ASSOCIATION FOR THE PROTECTION AND
PROMOTION OF AGRICULTURE
TO THE LANDOWNERS OF IRELAND
NO. 2

Tenakill, Abbeyleix, April 24

I think it right, my Lords and Gentlemen, to commence my present address by summing the statements of my preceding letter. It is requisite to preserve connexion and continuity. These are the statements I made: –

1. That the failure and famine have produced a dissolution of the form of social economy heretofore existing.
2. That society cannot possibly reassume its former sh[ape] and action.
3. That a new social state must either be formed, or be suffered to form itself; – in other words, that we must have either a *governed* or an *ungoverned* revolution.

‡ Lalor Papers, NLI MS 340, no. 58.

4. That the right and power of taking social existence in a new form reside, of necessity, in the great body of the people at large.

5. That for [the] sake of all classes, but more especially for their own, the landowners ought at once to take guidance of the revolution which is inevitable.

6. That they cannot do this effectively or safely otherwise than by placing themselves at the head of the people.

7. That the fundamental principle of association and united action must be that of distinct and declared allegiance to this, their native country.

8. That the formation of the 'Irish party' contains an involuntary admission of dependance on this island; but asserts no principle and affords no proof of allegiance or attachment.

9. That the constitution, resolutions, and proceedings of that party render it utterly worthless and inefficient for the purpose required, for any public purpose, or for its own professed or private objects.

10. That this Irish party should at once be re-constituted, enlarged, and extended; or another association be formed.

11. That the general object of the proposed association is that of framing and organising a new social constitution, based on sounder principles of ethics and economy than that which hitherto existed in this island.

12. That the object stated resolves itself into the establishment of an improved agricultural economy; and can be attained only by creating an independent and secure agricultural population.

13. That in the present circumstances of our condition, and until an affluent husbandry shall have first been created, no manufacture can be established on a secure foundation.

14. That the landowners are assuming and exercising the right of dictating and enforcing a new form and state of society for

the entire people of this kingdom, without asking counsel or aid, assent or acquiescence, from that people.

15. That the new social system which the landowners have adopted and are attempting to enforce, requires the extinction, by some process or other, of at least one-half the present existing people.

16. That this proceeding forces up the question of whether the eight thousand individuals who are owners of Ireland be of greater worth and heavier weight than the residual fraction of eight million people who are owners of nothing, – not even of their own lives; – and that, further, the success and safety of the proceeding may possibly depend on the practical solution of that question.

I am informed, and fear, that my assertion of our present incapacity to engage in manufacture will not be assented to by a large portion of the public. I would be desirous to prove my assertion at full; and to expose the prevalent error on this subject in every form of absurdity it can assume; but this I cannot do without more labour and loss of time than I can afford. Yet I cannot pass away from the point, for I think it of importance, without suggesting a few considerations, and soliciting attention to them.

That manufacturing, in a condensed and systematic form, can never rise and flourish in our condition of society; that small, rude, and scattered manufactures would be undersold and suppressed; and that it is therefore clearly impossible to establish or extend manufacture in Ireland on a scale sufficient to afford employment and subsistence to any considerable portion of its population until a material improvement shall have previously taken place in the general state of the country, and in the means and condition, more especially, of its agricultural classes; – this is the assertion I make.

If any one denies or doubts it, I beg of him to answer to himself, and to reflect before he answers, whether manufacturing activity and success be cause or consequence? Is it *ever* the cause, or ever any thing else than the effect of a productive and accumulating husbandry, and an extensive class of husbandmen, secured in the possession of subsistence, and of a large surplus beyond sub- sistence? Does manufacture ever precede and produce such a condition of husbandry or class of husbandmen? Is there argument or example to prove even the possibility? State the exact process and rationale of the process, the modus operandi, by which it accomplishes such a result. If you cannot do this, quote at least some example from the experience of history of such a result having been actually accomplished. Don't go to distant times or doubtful cases. Bring forward no dubious example, because I challenge the fact and the possibility. Of that mode of manufacture in which each house or village supplies itself of course I do not speak. I speak of the business of manufacturing as now understood and practised, – manufacturing for sale and trade, – manufacturing for the market; and I assert that in no country has that business ever risen and thriven whose agricultural condition was such as ours, that it is incompatible with such a condition; that in every country where it has flourished it was formed and supported by a secure and opulent husbandry; and that, finally, as a distinct and indepen- dent occupation it is never the cause, but always the consequence, of a high degree of general prosperity founded, in the first instance, on an abundant supply and surplus of food; and on the freedom, security, and ability enjoyed by the producers of that food in consuming, accumulating, and exchanging it. I might say more than this were it needful. I might say that general prosperity has prevailed in many countries where no manufacturing class was in distinct existence; but never in any country where the cultivators of the soil were in a low and depressed condition. But this is a fact that goes beyond my present object, and I have nothing to do with it. That, when a country is already rich and prosperous, a manufacturing system will greatly increase that prosperity, is also a fact that has nothing whatever to say in the present argument.

I challenge instance or example to disprove or disparage anything I have asserted; I could produce many to support and confirm. To name them would be to count all the countries in which the business of manufacturing has flourished. I will not refer to England or Scotland or Holland or Belgium, or any other of present or past days; but I point to Ulster and ask from whence rose the thriving manufacture of that province? It rose from a protected and prosperous husbandry; it rose under the guns [?] of yeomen-farmers. And why is it that no manufacture has been able to establish itself elsewhere in this island? That private enterprise has failed, and public effort been defeated? The want of a domestic Parliament? The act of Union? What! Is Ulster then not included in that act? Or included on other terms? And has Scotland, too, a home-parliament to foster or force her manufactures? She had an agriculture that gave her the means to make and maintain them.

But if you will repudiate general principles, and depart from the common course of nature and all nations, – if you will trample on reason, common sense, and experience, boldly aim at creating a precedent, and attempt to do what never was done before; yet still there are the special circumstances of our own peculiar case and condition to be taken in view and considered. Ireland, I freely admit, is not to be bound by the results of any preceding experiments or experience of other times or nations; nor fettered by the usual forms of any natural law of proceeding. She is certainly not to act as *Belgium* acted, but as *Ireland* is able and ought to act; and she may doubtless succeed where all others have failed. Her people, it is well known to all the world and to themselves, are the paragon and pattern-people of the earth. Let us limit the question, then, to the narrow ground, and look at the case under its own conditions and capabilities, without reference to former results. Ireland, you say, is able and ought at once to commence manufacturing, without watching or waiting longer for any development of agricultural prosperity, for any improvement in the general condition of the country, or for any increase of either its effective capital or of its market-power of consumption; nothing of which, indeed, can take effect or be created, until manufacture shall have first been established and put in action. Now, I request you to find out what is the amount of capital which an individual would require to possess in order to commence and carry on, against English competition, the manufacture of any one of the great articles of demand; and then to count up, for it will not be difficult, the names and number of all in Ireland who are known to possess that amount, disengaged and disposable. And which of them all will adventure to vest it in a manufacture, at the risque or rather certainty of ruin? Which of them, fearless for himself and forgetting his family, will kindle a furnace, or build a factory, in this country's cause for his country's sake? Good friends, – if manufactures could have safely been set on foot it would have been done long since. One of the strongest of our desires is the desire to make money, in Ireland as elsewhere; and if manufactures have not hitherto been established here, it is because, in a case like this, a single man with money at stake is wiser than mobs. No owner of capital in Ireland will adventure that capital on a manufacturing speculation merely because there is a mania in the public mind on the subject. But should he choose to try the adventure, then: – What is he to manufacture? What article can he make better and cheaper, finer and more finished, than England makes it?

Suppose himself fully competent to conduct, – educated, skilled, trained, practised – with what hands will he commence and continue? Irishmen? They are utterly unskilled. Teach and train them then. And lose his capital in training. English hands then. At English wages? They will not come. At higher wages then? What! In order to make a cheap article? But in England numbers are often thrown out of employment; and are seldom fully employed; – engage them. What! The bad hands, – the idle and drunken, – the refuse-workmen; for such are ever the men dismissed, or not fully employed. This in order to secure a superior article.

And for what market? Our own? he cannot depend on its capacity or its constancy, – he cannot depend on his own capital. There is no fixed and firm body of affluent farmers to give him the support of a steady market, such as the English manufacturer had when commencing; and an hundred Englishmen each with capital beyond his own, will combine to bear him down. A foreign market then. What market? None is open to him that is not open to the Englishman, and in occupation of the Englishman. The markets at her command are inadequate to employ the full productive power of England. The Irish manufacturer cannot sell the smallest quantity of goods without displacing the same quantity of English goods. Can he do so? Show a superior article, or sell a cheaper one? What advantage has he to enable or encourage him to make the attempt? None; but many disadvantages to discourage if not disable. All circumstances of condition that ever operated to prevent the growth of manufacture elsewhere are here in action; with one other circumstance added, more efficient than them all, – English competition. English manufacture would meet ours in every market to which it has access, and even in our own. English competition, conducted by an amount of ability, – of skill, capital, and trained energy, which would render a contest ruinous. Ireland, we are often told, has the manufacturing capacity, if she chose to use it; capital sufficient, and skill sufficient. True, – if Ireland sat alone by the sea. But the house across the way has capacity greater than ours. Ireland would have something more to do than simply to manufacture; – she would have to manufacture against England; and England is in possession. England preoccupies, with all the powers that ever attend preoccupation; and with almost unlimited capacity of production she holds possession of a limited market.

But we can have recourse to that very capacity; and turn a portion of English capital and skill against English interest and supremacy. Encourage and call on the English manufacturer to come here, settle, and set up his works. But will he come when you call? Why, and for what reasons should he come? Putting aside all reference to reasons of feeling, – personal attachments, social attractions, the habits of country, the affections of home, – there are yet many reasons why he should *not* come; and what reasons are there why he *should*? Suppose him to bring his stock, his machinery and apparatus, and his workmen; though all this would be neces- sary it would not be enough. All arts and manufactures advance together in equal step, and aid and support each other; and all these he should bring with him to put his own on the same footing it stood on in England; or leave it to stand alone and unsupported. It is not merely his own immediate workmen he would have to intro- duce; but the machinist, and mechanic, and artisan in ever branch of occupation necessary to the carrying on of his own immediate business, and of every other comprised or connected. Nor would this, nor all he could possibly do, be sufficient to supply or compen- sate the loss and want which he would daily and hourly feel of the thousand aids, appliances, and contrivances which the varied arts and universal skill of England have heaped round him on every hand; and which here are utterly wanting. He could not, of course, bring the facilities of communication and carriage which he has the benefit of in his own country. But why should he do all this, or any portion of it? Upon what reasons and motives should he come to this country even had he to bring but himself and his family? In order to obtain an Irish market? He has that market already at a trifling and still diminishing cost of carriage. This reason is in operation to induce him to carry his establishment to France, Belgium, Germany, and elsewhere, in order to place them beyond the custom-house; yet it is not very often, I believe, that he acts on it. Cheaper labour? Common labour is cheaper, but not any form of the labour which he would require. He would indeed be under lighter tax, and perhaps lower rent; but these are small items in the account. There was heretofore indeed, one advantage which this country enjoyed and had to offer; and which, if used and improved, might in time have created many more; – the cost of subsistence, more especially of food, was less than in England. Henceforth, I fear, this advantage will no longer exist. the operation of the measure abolishing the corn-duties will equalise the cost of food in the two countries, if it do not actually make it lower in England. Was it in order to strengthen and confirm the manufacturing success and supremacy of England that such pains were taken to neutralise Ireland on the question of the corn-laws?

There are doubtless several articles, but none of much general importance, the manufacture of which might be carried on even now in small establishments, scattered and isolated, with prospect of safety and success, when aided by great local advantages. Nothing I have said goes to deny this; or to deny that we are bound, each and all of us, on clear motives of individual interest as well as of social obligation, to give all the support we can afford, as customers and consumers, to every manufacture already established among us. But if any one whose mind is at his own command will take the pains to judge this question by consideration of the constant general causes and the actual special conditions, instead of allowing himself to be led by public fancies and follies, he will, I think, agree with me in asserting that until the support of an extensive and independent body of farmers shall have first been secured, no manufacture, able to cope and compete with that of England, can possibly be established and extended here, on a scale sufficient to change the general condition of the country, to create a market for the farmer, to increase the means and comforts of any class of society, or to afford employment and subsistence to any considerable portion of the population.

This present inability of Ireland to raise up a great manufacturing system is scarcely much to be regretted. In many respects and for many reasons no mode of employment can be less desirable for the mass of the people than that of manufacturing for a foreign market. Those reasons it is needless now to state; but I mean, and may have occasion, to state them thereafter. None of those reasons, however, stand in objection to the gradual establishment and development of manufactures for home-consumption, on a system of more intrinsic stability than the present English system, and with moral and economical securities which that system does not possess. Never, until a firm agricultural peasantry be created can any such system, or any system whatever, take action or existence in Ireland. An agricultural peasantry, – the only class that founds a people or forms a state; an agricultural peasantry, – the men alone who make a nation; an agricultural peasantry, – the single and sole foundation on which a social edifice can rise and rest that will not rock to every blast, and reel to the lightest blow; an agricultural peasantry, – not grass-farmers or gentlemen-farmers; not breeders of stock or feeders of fat cattle; not gentlemen who try to be farmers, nor farmers who try to be gentlemen. No such class as this, few in number and feeble in aggregate amount of means, with fine tastes and foreign fancies, can ever fill the place or fulfil the functions of a peasantry in helping to originate, excite, and nurture into stability the manufactures of Ireland. It is on a numerous, plain, and home-bred yeomanry alone the manufacturer can rely as efficient to support him. Should the scheme of consolidation be

successfully carried out, and Ireland become pasture-ground;
instead of being secured, enriched, and elevated, should the
present race of landholders be extinguished; should it be thought
more desirable to convert them into paupers than to make them
independent; should this be so, all help and hope for Irish manufacture is extinct for generations to come. Any one may convince
himself of this by considering the conditions under which a
manufacture commences, the steps and stages by which it advances
into stability, the process of its progression into perfection and
power. A great manufacturing system, such as dazzles our eyes in
England, takes the labour of generations to make. It cannot be
made to rise at once, nor built in a day; for this is a problem of
industrial progress which princes and parliaments have tried their
utmost strength upon, and never succeeded in solving yet. It must
itself be manufactured. It must be manufactured slowly, gradually,
painfully, – step by step, and stone by stone. It commences with
small means, small skill, and without a character. It is coarse-
handed, and liable to errors, more especially to errors of taste in
design and execution; deficient in contrivance, aptness, and
facility; in the tact and trick of trade. What it makes may possess
intrinsic value of strength and service; but wants shine and surface,
fineness and finish. The gaud and glitter are not on it. It acquires
all these by practice and success; it acquires them gradually; and
until it does acquire them it must depend altogether on the population of its own neighbourhood, county, or province; and mainly
on those classes of that population whose tastes and requirements
are not fastidious or refined; whose demand is for the article in its
common and coarse form; and whose effective consumption is the
greatest in aggregate amount. This is the upward road that every
manufacture must travel, – that all manufactures have travelled
that ever rose into greatness. This is the *upward* road, – but there is
a *downward* road too. When an Irish manufacturer with capital and

credit to the amount of some few thousands, and skill enough to make a sound and serviceable but coarse article, – when, without a single advantage of all the Englishman possesses; – without his established character and connection, finished skill, knowledge of trade, practised facility, tried conductors and managers, trained and picked working hands, a wealthy native market, an effective foreign agency, all science and arts, inventive genius, adaptive talent, and social arrangements working to aid him; – when without one of these, or a thousand advantages beside, the Irishman boldly or blindly undertakes to manufacture a fine article for a foreign market which is preoccupied and glutted, or a coarse article for a native market which does not exist; and in either case to manufacture, not against the Englishman but against all England, for all England will bend its united force to bear him out of the market; – this is the downward road, the road to ruin; and this is the road he is often and loudly encouraged and called on to take. Good friends! who talk of Ireland's material resources, manufacturing capacity, and trading facilities; and who are ever exhorting us to use and apply them under impossible conditions, will you give your aid to alter those conditions? Will you, more especially, give aid in creating what is the first and indispensable requisite, and which, if created, will create all the rest – and independent and affluent tillage-husbandry; a husbandry in the hands of yeomen-farmers[?]. Remember it is not the town that makes the country; it is the country that makes the town. Make the market, the market will make the manufacture.

On this very prevalent idea that a manufacturing system is the efficient cause, instead of being merely, as it is, the consequence and product, of general and agricultural prosperity, I have stated my opinion at more length than I intended; or than might seem necessary to my immediate object. Yet I have not been writing without a purpose, though that purpose may not at once appear.

I have said that manufacturing conditions can never take effect where agriculture is poor and depressed; and that with us, therefore, agricultural progress is necessary to manufacturing development. I say further that no manufacturing system whatever is necessary to advance agriculture into positive and full independence, and a condition at least of comparative wealth. Of this no particular statement in proof is required. I merely remark, in order to remind you of the fact. For every one must recollect the many countries in all times where scarcely a single article of manufacture was ever made *for sale*; and which yet attained, as many still enjoy, a very high state of agricultural and general prosperity. Whether such countries – where no mighty manufacturing establishments rise and range in sets and systems round some general and gigantic centre; where no furnace or factory denaturalises the very elements, or makes the soul of man to shrink and sink, shrivel and snivel into the soul of a slubber, a cropper, or a pin-maker; but where every house or hamlet manufactures for itself; – whether such countries may not possess the greater share of real and true prosperity, of public and private virtue, elevation of character and feeling, material and moral security, natural dignity of condition, mental health and physical health, and, in a word, of true general happiness, – this is a question I have no concern with. I have stated, I think, enough to enable any man to convince himself that in order to fulfil and effect what I believe, my Lords and Gentlemen, to be your first duty and your chief desire, the creation of an improved and prosperous state and condition of Ireland, the establishment of a new and amended social constitution, there is one principle of action, one mode of proceeding, one direction and course of movement; and but one alone. To you, and not alone to you, nor to any of the classes who live by direct labour on the land, but also to those who, either from personal interest or public motives, look to manufactures for subsistence, or look to them as a chief and desirable source of employment and mode of industry to the people of Ireland, – even for [the] sake of securing a chance of that manufacturing system they covet, to them as well as to you and to us there ought to be but one object now, and one path of united effort; – that of saving from destruction, protecting, and promoting our domestic agriculture; and of placing it on a footing it never yet stood upon in Ireland, the footing of perfect social independence. And if, by any labour of mine, I can succeed in withdrawing the forces that exist in this island from the thousand devious and diverging paths, leading nowhere, into which they have so long been distracted, where effort is wasted, energy dissipates, and the pride of man and country takes disgust, – if I can succeed in inducing them, leagued and linked, to bend and bear in this one path on this one point, – then indeed and assuredly my labour will not have been lost.

The formation of an active, productive, and independent tillage-husbandry is then the only means to which Ireland can look forward with any real and rational hope, – with any hope that can stand one cool moment's examination, – of deliverance from her present state of poverty, disturbance, and insecurity; of the establishment, on a settled and solid basis, of tranquillity, industry, order, and prosperity; of the creation, in a word, of happier and more elevated social conditions than those hitherto existing. To form such a system of husbandry ought therefore to be made the sole object of all classes now; and it is one that can be easily and safely effected only by the united power of the landed proprietors combined and acting, in some organised mode, or form of association, with the combined power of the general people, – more particularly that portion of the people who form the class of tenant-cultivators. It is most unwise and unjust to be looking ever and altogether to government; in a case like the present more especially. Government can do much; but there are things which governments cannot do, – which men must do for themselves, or leave undone; and this is one of them. It is vain and useless to be looking always to Parliament. It is only in a legal sense that Parliament is omnipotent; there are things which Parliaments cannot do, and this is one of them. It is worse than vain to be looking – as too many in Ireland are looking – to what is called Agitation. There are things which Agitation cannot do; which are too hot and too heavy for it to do; and there are things which it dare not do; and among those which it cannot and dare not do, are the very things which are now required to be done. It is not a *destructive*, but a *creative* and *conservative* agency that is wanted now. It is, I fear, just as vain to look now to the landed proprietors, acting as individuals. The condition of Ireland is beyond the competency of isolated private exertion. Things are wanting to be done which individuals cannot do, and will not undertake or attempt to do. It is not unconnected acts but a system of measures that can now be efficient. To save their country and themselves it is necessary that the landowners should now at length exert the full power they possess; that they should act instantly and earnestly; and that they should act as a body, collectively and simultaneously, upon common principles and for a common purpose. That they should so act has long been, I think, what prudent and energetic men would have considered a necessity. The sort of necessity which forces men to act whether they will or no, or sink and surrender to it, has now at length arrived, to arouse or to abolish them.

The formation of the Agricultural society seems in some degree to recognise the necessity for combined exertion in any attempt to improve agriculture; and the fruitlessness of trusting to unconnected individual efforts. If I considered that society to be efficacious in any degree I might think it needless to address you. But whatever it might be able to effect in ordinary times, it is useless now, and has, to all practical intent, been altogether abolished by the crisis. Its only common sense proceeding now would be to adjourn to May, 1850. There are obstacles to the improvement of husbandry, and dangers threatening its very existence, which that society can do nothing to remove or avert. Another association is required; an association for protection and preservation, as well as for promotion and progress. Call that association, my Lords and Gentlemen, by what name you will; a Convocation of estates, a national assembly, an Irish party, an agricultural association; it matters not for the name, – but in some such association or assembly will you meet the people of Ireland, and make an amicable settlement of the several questions that have long been in debate between you and them, and which now threaten to come to a deadly quarrel?

The circumstances which, I think, render such an association requisite are the following: –

1. Failure of the potato.

2. Free admission of foreign corn.

3. Arrangements between landlord and tenant.

4. General feeling of hostility between the classes of landowner and occupier.

5. Political agitation.

6. The Middleman.

These are the circumstances which call for an amicable settlement by voluntary agreement between the landed proprietors and the people at large in association assembled. There are some few others, but those I have enumerated are the chief. In the present letter I can [do] nothing more than merely mention them. In another, and some few subsequent letters, I may possibly state and examine them in detail.

I have the honor to remain &c.

James F. Lalor

Select Bibliography

PRIMARY SOURCES

I. MANUSCRIPTS

British Library
Peel Papers Addenda, MS 40530

National Archives of Ireland
Official Papers
Outrage Reports, Tipperary

National Library of Ireland
C. G. Duffy Papers, MS 5757
Lalor Family Papers, MSS 8563, 8570
Lalor Papers, MS 340

II. OFFICIAL PUBLICATIONS

33 Geo. III, c.29, *An Act to prevent the Election or Appointment of unlawful assemblies, under pretence of preparing or presenting public Petitions or other Addresses to His Majesty, or the Parliament.*
Second report from the Select Committee of the House of Lords, appointed to inquire into the collection and payment of tithes in Ireland, and the state of the laws relating thereto; with the minutes of evidence, and an appendix, and index. 1831–2.

III. PUBLISHED WORKS BY CONTEMPORARIES

Conner, William, *True Political Economy of Ireland* (Dublin, 1835).
O'Connell, Daniel, *Observations on Corn Laws; On Political Pravity and Ingratitude; and on Clerical and Personal Slander, in the Shape of a Meek and Modest Reply to the Second Letter of the Earl of Shrewsbury, Waterford, and Wexford, to Ambrose Lisle Phillipps, Esq.* (Dublin, 1842).

IV. NEWSPAPERS

Chicago Tribune
Irish Felon
Irish Nation
Irish News
Irish People (Dublin)
Irishman (Dublin)
Nation
Nenagh Guardian
The Times
Tipperary Vindicator
Tribune (Dublin)

SECONDARY SOURCES

I. BOOKS AND PAMPHLETS

Bourke, Marcus, *John O'Leary: A Study in Irish Separatism* (Tralee, 1967).
Boyce, D. George, *Nineteenth-Century Ireland: The Search for Stability* (Dublin, 1990).
Buckley, David N., *James Fintan Lalor: Radical* (Cork, 1990).
Collected Works of Padraic H. Pearse: Political Writings and Speeches (Dublin, n. d.).
Connolly, James, *Labour in Irish History* (New York, 1919).
Davitt, Michael, *The Fall of Feudalism in Ireland* (London and New York, 1904).
Donnelly, James S., *Captain Rock: The Irish Agrarian Rebellion of 1821–1824* (Madison and Dublin, 2009).
Duffy, Charles Gavan, *My Life in Two Hemispheres* (2 vols, London, 1898).
Fogarty, Lilian, *James Fintan Lalor: Patriot and Political Essayist, 1807–1849* (Dublin, 1918).

Gray, Peter, *Famine, Land and Politics: British Government and Irish Society 1843–50* (Dublin, 1999).

Kerr, Donal A., *'A Nation of Beggars?' Priests, People, and Politics in Famine Ireland 1846–1852* (Oxford, 1994).

Lee, J. Joseph, *The Modernisation of Irish Society, 1848–1918* (Dublin, 1973).

Leech, Henry Brougham, *1848 and 1887: The Continuity of the Irish Revolutionary Movement* (London, 1887).

Leighton, C. D. A., *The Irish Manufacture Movement, 1840–1843*, Maynooth Historical Series, no. 5 (Maynooth, 1987).

Moody, T. W., *Davitt and Irish Revolution, 1846–82* (Oxford, 1981).

O'Hanlon, John, Edward O'Leary and Matthew Lalor, *History of the Queen's County* (II, Dublin, 1907–14).

O'Neill, Thomas P., *James Fintan Lalor*, trans. John T. Goulding (Dublin, 2003).

Quinn, James, *John Mitchel*, UCD Press Life and Times New Series (Dublin, 2009).

The Writings of James Fintan Lalor, The Shamrock Library (Dublin, 1895).

II. ARTICLES

Breen, Aidan, 'The history and administration of the Gorey Poor Law Society 1840–49: A case-study in the operations of the Irish Poor Law, *The Past: The Organ of the Uí Cinsealaigh Historical Society*, No. 28 (2007), pp. 43–74.

Gambles, Anna, 'Rethinking the politics of protection: conservatism and the corn laws, 1830–52', *The English Historical Review*, vol. 113, no. 453 (Sept., 1998), pp. 928–52.

Lusztig, Michael, 'Solving Peel's puzzle: repeal of the corn laws and institutional preservation', *Comparative Politics*, vol. 27, no. 4 (July, 1995), pp. 393–408.

Newman, Jeremiah, 'The priests of Ireland: a socio-religious survey. I. Numbers and distribution', *The Irish Ecclesiastical Record*, vol. xcviii, no. 5 (1962), pp. 1–27.

O'Brien, George, 'William Conner', *Studies: An Irish Quarterly Review*, vol. 12, no. 46 (June, 1923), pp. 279–89.

O'Donoghue, Patrick, 'Causes of the opposition to tithes, 1830–38', *Studia Hibernica*, no. 5 (1965), pp. 7–28.

_____, 'Opposition to tithe payments in 1830–31', *Studia Hibernica*, no. 6 (1966), pp. 69–98.

O'Neill, Thomas P., 'The Irish land question, 1830–1850', *Studies: An Irish Quarterly Review*, vol. 44, no. 175 (autumn, 1955), pp. 325–36.